Missions Most Secret

MISSIONS
MOST SECRET
GRAEME COOK

HARWOOD-SMART PUBLISHING

First published in Great Britain 1976 by
HARWOOD-SMART PUBLISHING CO LTD
Wessex House Blandford Heights Blandford Dorset DT11 7TS
and
18 Coulson Street Chelsea London SW3 3NB

ISBN 0 904507 17 3

Text set in 12 pt Photon Times, printed by photolithography,
and bound in Great Britain at The Pitman Press, Bath

Contents

Acknowledgements   vii

Introduction   ix

1   The Phantom Raiders   1

2   Shepherds of the Invasion   35

3   Terror from the Skies   72

4   The Impostors   109

5   Baltic Episode   145

Bibliography   186

For Paul, my son

Acknowledgements

The author wishes to express his most sincere gratitude to those authors and publishers who gave their permission to draw upon their books and magazines for background information. I should also like to express my appreciation of the assistance given by the Ministry of Defence (Army, Air and Navy), the Director and Staff of the Imperial War Museum, London, the Staff of the Chester public libraries, Felicity Harwood-Smart, my Publisher, and Julia Brittain, my Editor, but especially to Fidelma for her encouragement and inspiration.

Introduction

On a starlit night in March 1941, His Majesty's submarine *Triumph* nosed towards the Greek Island of Rhodes. She slipped across the surface, barely disturbing a calm sea. In the conning tower, which jutted like a fat finger from the slender deck, the captain calmly issued clipped orders, barely audible over the steady hum of the submarine's electric motors. His voice was steady and authoritative, betraying no hint of the tension he was surely feeling as he nursed the boat steadily closer to the enemy-held spread of land ahead.

Beneath him in the control room two men stood waiting for the 'green light'—the order from the young skipper that would send them on a mission so secret that its discovery by the enemy would mean catastrophe for an entire invasion force. The appearance of the two men could only be described as comic, but no-one was laughing. Their lives and possibly those of many others were at stake. Their eyes shone white from their blackened faces. Each wore a thick sweater daubed with grease, and their clown-like apparel was completed by long underwear, also coated with grease. They had with them torches, pistols and various paraphernalia for reconnaissance. These two young men, one a naval officer, the other a commando, were about to pave the way for an amphibious invasion of the island. Three years later that same naval officer was to shepherd to its goal the mightiest armada of naval craft ever assembled. Without him and the small band of men he recruited to help him, D-day, the invasion of Europe, might well have ended in disaster.

In both the great wars of this century men have embarked upon operations whose secrecy was paramount to their success. Not all of them were spies, indulging in acts of espionage. There were those who played a dangerous game of bluff by manning innocent-looking tramp steamers during World War One. They plied the sea lanes of the Atlantic, setting themselves up as targets for marauding German U-boats. But behind the innocent exterior lay a sting that was to sound the death knell for many an unsuspecting U-boat crew.

The First World War was barely over when a young naval lieutenant was summoned to the office of the chief of Britain's Secret Intelligence Service. He was despatched on a mission that was to culminate in one of the great events of British Naval history and earn him his country's highest award for valour. The veil of secrecy was drawn tight over Lieutenant Augustus Agar's escapade. Indeed, the reason for his high award was known only to a privileged few.

When the Allied and Axis armies became locked in conflict on the barren wastes of the Western Desert during the Second World War, air supcriority became a crucial factor in deciding the issue. A towering, lean Scots Guards captain on loan to the commandos formed a group which engaged in clandestine operations behind enemy lines. He and his band of saboteurs 'subtracted' more aircraft from the enemy air strength than did all the fighter aeroplanes of the Allied air forces in the desert. Dubbed the 'Phantom Major', this young Scot gave birth to the Special Air Service, an élite Army corps which in recent years has attracted a more sinister notoriety.

In 1944 Hitler unleashed waves of pilotless flying bombs against the cities of southern England in a last-ditch effort to bring Britain to her knees and reverse his fortunes in the course of the war. Had it not been for the determined efforts of courageous underground and resistance workers, notably in France and Poland, he might have succeeded. A secret agent operating in France brilliantly pieced together a jumble of seemingly innocuous and unconnected facts. The result was the discovery of a whole string of launching pads for Hitler's 'revenge weapons' which were designed to reduce London to ruins. The Royal Air Force nipped that venture in the bud. Meanwhile a young Polish teacher doing forced labour in a German factory caught a fleeting glimpse of a pilotless 'aeroplane' while engaged in cleaning duties. He mentioned this to a member of the Polish underground and that chance sighting brought about the discovery of the German V-1 flying bomb. Even more terrifying was its successor, the V-2 rocket. Here again the Poles demonstrated their expertise in the art of espionage which resulted in one of the most dramatic discoveries of the war.

In both World Wars carefully contrived surprise actions often proved to be the most potent weapon in the Allied armoury. The need to maintain absolute secrecy in such situations often gave rise to more tension in the preparatory stages than did the operation itself. One false word, one innocent whisper in the wrong place, one minor oversight could—and so tragically often did—spell disaster.

For those who courageously ventured into enemy territory upon secret missions, a swift death by the bullet was a merciful end. More often than not, if caught, they were subjected to the most sickening torture before being killed. Theirs must have been the most supreme courage, for they knew that this awful fate awaited them if they were betrayed or chanced to fall into enemy hands. This dreadful hazard they accepted with a courage that humbled all others. But they were by no means superhuman; rather they were ordinary men and women fired by patriotism, a devotion to duty or a loathing for the enemy.

It would be impossible to assess the extent to which these clandestine operators influenced the outcome of war. What is undeniably true is that countless Allied soldiers, sailors, airmen and civilians owe their lives to the courage of these men and women. Their efforts doubtless enabled the massed forces of the Allies to shorten the war.

Contained within this book are five stories, each different from the others, but all with the same underlying theme: the absolute secrecy essential for the success of the operations. Perhaps these true accounts will give the reader an insight into the great spirit of those who ventured forth on 'Missions Most Secret'.

1

The Phantom Raiders

The black embrace of darkness cloaked the RAF base at
Heliopolis in Egypt one night in 1941. Fighter and bomber aircraft sat squat and motionless, dispersed around the apron of the
hard, sandy expanse that formed the airfield. A gentle but bitingly
cold wind breathed across the airfield, finding its way into the
crevices on the aircraft, composing and performing a symphony
of eerie whistles, barely audible to the sentries who paced their
'beats'. The sentries were alert and on edge, their nerves taut in
expectation. They had been warned to expect intruders and they
were ready for them. The slightest unusual sound brought a
challenge—but no reply. Their eyes were playing them false. In
the jet, brooding shadows of the aircraft there were occasional
stirs but quick investigations revealed nothing.

Throughout the previous few days, RAF aircraft had scoured
the desert regions near Heliopolis, seeking out a small group of
men bent on 'raiding' their airfield. Nothing suspicious had been
seen. It seemed that there was to be no raid after all. The 'hawks'
had uncovered nothing out of the ordinary in the shady and rocky
wastes of the desert; no tell-tale tracks, no movement to give the
intruders away. But they had been there . . .

The hours of darkness passed and as the sun rose like a giant
ball of fire, the sentries shook the cold from their bodies. The anticipated raid would not come now; not in daylight. They sighed in
relief. They had done their job—now it was time for a well-earned
rest. As one of them made to leave his group of charges, he idly
patted the fuselage of an aircraft.

'Safe as bloody 'ouses, wi' us around,' he muttered to himself.
But his confident proclamation had hardly left his lips when he
stopped in his tracks. Stuck on the side of the aircraft was a label
bearing the word 'DESTROYED'.

'What the bloody hell—' he began. Then the awful realisation dawned. He bolted across to another aircraft parked nearby. It bore a similar label. Then on to another—and another. All the same.

'Oh Christ!' he exclaimed. 'The C.O. will have my guts for this . . . But I didn't see a bloomin' thing!'

He was not the only one. After a close inspection had been carried out, no fewer than forty-five aircraft were found to have been 'destroyed'. The Commanding Officer, a Group Captain, was 'displeased'. If these labels had been bombs, he'd have been minus forty-five aeroplanes—probably more. But there was another reason for his anger. He had lost ten pounds as a result of that 'raid'. A few days earlier he had accepted a bet that a certain young commando officer, aided by a group of newly-trained saboteurs, could not penetrate his airfield. The field was so well guarded that such an attack was thought impossible. But that night that same commando, along with thirty-nine of his men, had been and gone.

One of the most alarming features of the raid was that, despite the intensive RAF reconnaissance carried out before it, the saboteurs had marched no less than ninety miles across the very expanse of desert which the RAF had searched with such diligence—and had not been seen. All forty of them had made the trip on foot, marching in the bitter cold of the desert night and sleeping by day, concealed by their own cunningly-devised camouflage. All this was topped by the attack itself during which not a single soul on the airfield realised that forty raiders were scurrying around their aircraft planting 'bombs'. The success of the raid left the Group Captain speechless. Thereafter, security at the airfield was tightened up.

The Commando Lieutenant who had made the rash boast was a mountainous, athletic Scotsman by the name of David Stirling. A quietly spoken man, he was gentle by nature, but this outward placidity belied a man of extraordinary vigour, an adventurer and one who was to give birth to and lead the most potent and secret small raiding force of the entire Second World War.

Before the outbreak of war, Stirling had been in the American Rocky Mountains, toning up and training for an assault upon the highest peak in the world, Mount Everest. It was typical of the man that he should have set his sights upon a goal which most men thought unconquerable. Everest was a challenge and Stirling was at his best when the odds were weighted against him. But then his training was interrupted by the outbreak of the war in 1939. This was an even greater challenge and he returned to Great Britain where he joined the Scots Guards. The choice of regiment was automatic, because two of his three brothers were already serving officers in it.

With an ingrained sense of adventure goading him on to get into the fray with the enemy, Stirling went through his training with unbridled impatience. He was a man of action and although his training did have its moments of excitement, he was keen to get on with the 'real thing'. Instructional classes were a bore and he showed it by often falling asleep during lectures, much to the chagrin of his instructors. However, a chance encounter with a fellow officer was to remedy the malaise of inactivity.

The meeting took place in a London club where Stirling got into conversation with Major Robert Laycock, who was at that time recruiting officers for the newly-formed Number 8 Commando. Stirling's eyes lit up at the prospect of commando operations and Laycock quickly sensed that he had a willing recruit. A handshake did it and soon Stirling found himself undergoing the most rigorous training the Army could devise.

When his training was complete, Stirling was en route for the Middle East. Laycock, by then a colonel, had amassed a force of five commando units to be known as 'Layforce', which was to do battle with the Axis forces in North Africa and the Mediterranean theatre. But the nature of the war being fought in that area did not lend itself easily to large-scale commando operations and Layforce was eventually disbanded. As a result Stirling found himself in Alexandria, redundant and impatiently awaiting fresh orders. He had already seen many of his brother officers posted back to Britain and he did not relish the thought of being taken from what was at that time the main battle zone. There seemed little prospect of a tangle with the enemy back in Britain.

During these days of waiting he reflected upon the fate of Layforce. Stirling reasoned, quite rightly, that its failure was due to its lack of mobility and to its size. There were other contributory factors, but these were the basic ones. Commandos, he conjectured, would be most effectively employed if they operated in small, highly mobile units, striking at the enemy from behind its own lines, hitting hard and swiftly, then retreating when the damage was done, leaving the enemy confused by the lightning attack. In Stirling's estimation, secrecy and surprise were paramount elements.

It was while he was engrossed in these thoughts that he chanced to hear that another officer in the Number 8 Commando, one 'Jock' Lewes, had 'fallen heir' to a consignment of parachutes which, by some clerical error, had inadvertently been delivered to Alexandria. It happened that at that time there wasn't a spare parachute to be had in North Africa. Lewes had struck gold, and Stirling pounced with the alacrity of a hungry prospector.

J. S. 'Jock' Lewes was one of those who had come to the Middle East with Layforce. An officer in the Welsh Guards, he, like Stirling, was a man of incredible foresight and, as we shall see, the concerted brain-power of these two men was to have a considerable effect upon the war in the desert. To Lewes, a problem was merely a challenge to be overcome and he loved unravelling them. He was a studious person, an Australian who had come to England and studied at Christ Church College, Oxford, where he distinguished himself reading philosophy, politics and economics; not, one might think, essential prerequisites for becoming a commando. But in addition to his academic pursuits at university, Lewes shone as President of the Oxford University Boat Club. A superb athlete, he gained a rowing 'blue' and gave Oxford her first victory over Cambridge, her old adversary, after a succession of defeats.

Even before Stirling tracked down Lewes, the Australian's thoughts had already been working along the same lines as Stirling's. The acquisition of the parachutes was a piece of extremely good fortune and Lewes meant to put them to good use. It appeared that they had been destined for India. With Laycock's connivance, Lewes ensured that they never did reach their original destination.

As he raced to see Lewes to cast an eye upon his prize, Stirling saw that the parachutes might be the answer to his prayers and 'bale him out' of his interlude of inactivity. If he could raise a commando unit that could be dropped by parachute behind the enemy lines, he could give the enemy the fright of its life by attacking from within its own territory.

Lewes was fascinated by Stirling's embryonic idea and willingly contributed his precious parachutes. But there was a problem. There was not only a shortage of parachutes but an even greater dearth of precious aircraft. The only one Stirling could 'borrow' was a somewhat outdated Valentia, almost totally unsuited to the task of dropping parachutists. To him, however, that was a minor difficulty which could be overcome. So it was that he recruited six 'sky divers'. But that was not all. Jumping for the first time from an ancient aircraft not properly equipped to take 'static lines' was one thing. To do it without any previous instruction was quite another. To his horror, Stirling discovered that there was not a single parachute instructor in the whole of North Africa. His attitude was typical—'So what? Nothing is perfect in war!'

Stirling and his intrepid band of fledgelings made their way to the airfield at Mersa Matruh where they clambered aboard the tired old Valentia and the cranky aircraft lumbered along the runway and struggled into the air. This particular aircraft was designed for passengers—and not the sort who intended leaping out of its door in mid-flight!

Since there were no proper connections for their static line attachments, which were designed to open the parachute automatically after the parachutist had jumped, Stirling and his budding bird men were obliged to improvise. They simply clipped their static lines onto the metal legs of the passenger seats.

The Valentia clawed its way higher into the clear blue sky over the desert. When, after what seemed like an interminable period, it had reached a safe height, the aircraft approached the dropping zone and the door was hauled open. The sudden draught of air caused by the slip stream almost bowled them all over but Stirling fought his way against it and stood in the open doorway, gripping its edges and probably regretting the mad impulse that had prompted him to get involved in such a dangerous and precarious pursuit. He glanced down at the desert below then, gritting his teeth, he leapt out into mid-air. Almost instantly there was a tug at his back as the static line on the parachute jerked it open. The white silk spilled out—too soon. The billowing canopy caught in the tail-plane of the aircraft as Stirling fell away and for a fraction of a second he was held fast. He glanced back to see the white silk begin to tear. It ripped open until suddenly he was free and falling. With the parachute only partially open, Stirling hurtled earthwards gathering speed as he plummeted down. This was the sort of experience that few men ever survived to relate. It was Stirling's first jump—and it looked like being his very last.

Terrified, he struggled to gain control of the 'chute as the air sped through the widening gap in the canopy. But down he fell at increased speed until the ground seemed to rocket up towards him. He hit it with a jarring thud. Then, oblivion.

Stirling was badly injured but miraculously he was alive. He was rushed to hospital where it was found that a back injury had paralysed both his legs. For three weeks he lay in bed, unable to move the lower part of his body. But his injuries did not extend to his very active brain which was working at a furious pace. He spent every waking hour planning, formulating in his mind the germ of an idea—a new-style commando unit. He pored over maps of the Western Desert, developing an intimacy with its every contour, line of communication, enemy and allied position. No detail was missed and he encapsulated his ideas in a memorandum which he intended to submit to no less a personage than the Commander-in-Chief himself.

His period of incapacity allowed him the opportunity to examine the war situation in the North African theatre. He pinpointed the areas at which the enemy was most vulnerable; on his coastal communication route, his transport parks, airfields and myriad other targets, most of which lay at or near the coast. He recognised the paramount importance of surprise in any commando operation. He judged that one of the prime reasons for Layforce's failure had been due in no small measure to the massive size of the raiding parties involved in missions. He concluded therefore that the element of surprise could more easily be achieved if the group carrying out the attack was small and as a result less likely to be seen by the defenders. Amphibious commando raids had, in the past, not met with great success in North Africa. The right sort of boats had not been employed.

His thesis concluded that a handful of men could effect as much, if not more, damage and achieve greater strike power than could a large force of commandos. That, basically, was it, and he committed those thoughts to paper. He even made suggestions as to how the raids should be carried out: either from the air, over land or, if possible, by sea, although in these initial stages and despite his misfortune in his first jump, he favoured the parachute. He earmarked potential targets, bearing in mind that a major offensive was planned for the not too distant future. A multitude of other details were included in what was a brief exposition; training, types of weapons and bombs to be used and the number of officers and men he would require.

After several weeks in hospital, Stirling was hobbling around the ward on crutches, itching to put his new plan forward for consideration. Alas he had seen other bright ideas submitted only to get lost amid a mountain of red tape and he vowed that a similar fate was not to befall his scheme. He would go right to the top—and there was no time like the present. So, on a bright July day in 1941, the crippled commando lurched out of the hospital, defying doctors in their bid to 're-capture' him, and bundled himself into a car which he pointed in the direction of the Middle East Headquarters, Cairo.

In planning his tactics for the new unit, Stirling had foreseen difficulties with keen-eyed sentries standing sentinel over enemy installations. But he had not anticipated that the first belligerent sentry he would encounter would be British. Stirling drew up at the gates of the headquarters building and was informed politely but firmly by the sentry that since he had no pass he would not be allowed in. Stirling tried everything in the book to persuade the resolute private to let him pass, but the young soldier would have none of it. Despondent, but still determined, Stirling retreated to allow some legitimate visitors to go through the gateway. It occurred to him that his plan to evade enemy sentries and blow up their aircraft and other installations would hardly look convincing if he could not get past a friendly one!

Divesting himself of his crutches, he slipped through a narrow gap between the sentry box and the high fence which encircled the headquarters. He was through. As he hobbled as fast as he could towards the door to the building, he could almost feel the sentry's eyes upon him. His instinct proved right.

'Stop that man!' the sentry bellowed.

But Stirling launched himself through the door, determined to reach his goal. Once inside, he made off along a corridor as fast as his weakened legs would carry him. He knew that by now they would be after him. Then he saw a door marked 'Adjutant General'. This would do, he thought, in desperation. Without bothering to knock, he opened the door and walked in—then stopped dead in his tracks. Had Stirling known who was on the other side of that door, he would have chosen another.

Sitting at a desk, looking fiery with anger, his eyes ablaze at the intrusion, was an Army major Stirling knew of old. There was no love lost between them.

The major glowered at Stirling in disbelief as he recognised him. He remembered that same young man falling asleep during one of his lectures while Stirling was under training with the Scots Guards. Stirling had been tired after a hectic binge the night before—or had it been sheer boredom?

The lanky subaltern apologised for his unceremonious entry and explained that he had come to see the C-in-C, General Auchinleck, on business of the utmost importance. He attempted to explain to the major the outline of his plan for the commando unit, but his garbled explanation fell upon deaf ears. The major showed his interest by bidding Stirling a curt 'good day'.

As Stirling backed out of the door, the major's 'phone rang and the snippet of conversation that Stirling heard telegraphed to him the news that the alarm had been raised. That was all he had to hear. He closed the door and lurched off farther down the corridor. At last he came to another door. He drew a deep breath and opened it. There before him sat a man he recognised but had never met before, General Neil Ritchie, the Deputy Chief of Staff, Middle-East Forces. Stirling was as near to the top now as he'd ever get and he reckoned that the result of his intrusion could be either a court martial or a hearing. He muttered an apology but hurriedly explained that he had urgent business with Auchinleck.

Ritchie eyed the young Scot towering over his desk and told him to sit. As he lowered himself into the chair, Stirling handed the General his memorandum. It was written in longhand and Ritchie clearly had difficulty in deciphering Stirling's scrawl but he studied what was written very carefully. Stirling watched the General for some reaction as he read but there was none. At last Ritchie laid it down on the desk in front of him and looked up.

'You know, Stirling, this might be just the sort of thing we've been looking for. Leave this with me and I'll discuss it with the Commander-in-Chief. You'll have his decision within the next few days.'

Stirling was taken aback. He had not reckoned on Ritchie reacting so favourably so soon and his excitement must have been obvious to the senior officer. He expressed his thanks but the

General interrupted.

'If you get the go-ahead on this project, there is one man who will have to help you with the administration side of the operation, my Adjutant General. I think you'd better meet him now.'

With that Ritchie lifted one of his telephones and summoned the Adjutant to his office. Moments later the door opened and there stood the major with whom Stirling had crossed swords earlier. A look of utter amazement crossed the major's face when he saw Stirling reclining in the General's guest chair. Stirling could not restrain a slight smirk of satisfaction.

Ritchie introduced the two men and Stirling intimated that they had already met. With that, Ritchie bade them good day and the two men left the room. Once outside in the corridor, however, the major made it clear to Stirling that he would do all that duty required of him—but no more. The young lieutenant knew then that he was in for a rough ride and would have to tread very carefully in his dealings with the major. He was to find out only too soon just how difficult that major could be.

General Ritchie was not the kind of man to waste time when he had before him a scheme that looked good and he immediately put forward the plan to Auchinleck, another Scot, who gave the project his blessing.

Three days after his interview with Ritchie, Stirling was ordered to report to general headquarters to see Auchinleck himself and he was formally given the 'green light' to go ahead. The General told him that he could recruit six officers and sixty men and that they were to set up a base in the Suez Canal zone. There he would have to organise a crash training course in readiness for a raid on German airfields on the night before Auchinleck intended launching a major offensive against the enemy. Stirling was to take the rank of captain and the unit under his command would be known as 'L Detachment' of the Special Air Service.

The Special Air Service was in fact non-existent, an imaginary force set up to fool the enemy into thinking there was a para-military force in the Middle East capable of launching attacks on them. Now, under Stirling's command, the SAS was to become a reality.

Excitement welled within Stirling at the prospect of forming the new unit and getting into the fray. But he was almost immediately faced with problems. Picking the right men for the job was to be his greatest headache. He had already drawn up a short-list of officers and men he wanted but he knew he would encounter difficulty in getting their release. More difficult than getting the men, however, was obtaining supplies. The Adjutant General had wasted no time in spreading the word that Stirling was *persona non grata*, and when the eager young Scot requested equipment for the unit he found himself bogged down in the inevitable morass of red tape. He was told in no uncertain terms that he would have to wait his turn in the queue, no matter how urgent his needs. Stirling decided that if he could not get the goods he wanted by fair means then he would indulge in a little piracy. For the time being however, he focused his attentions upon recruiting the men who would make up the first unit of the Special Air Service.

Jock Lewes was an obvious choice. His ability as an organiser was well known, and Stirling was in dire need of such a man. Lewes was followed by an Irishman called McGonigal, a Scot, Bill Fraser, and two Englishmen, Thomas and Bonnington. Then Stirling searched around for suitable NCOs and persuaded men like Cooper, Seekings, Rose, Bennet and Lilley to join him.

There was yet another officer he was more than keen to get but he was to encounter some difficulty in getting him. He was at that time under close arrest, having struck his Commanding Officer after a disagreement. The miscreant was R. B. Mayne, a giant of a man who hailed from Ulster. Before the war, he had been an international rugby player but with the outbreak of hostilities he had exchanged the rugby scrum for an even more dangerous one. Stirling had to use all his persuasive powers to convince Mayne's C.O. that the bellicose lieutenant was urgently required for work of great secrecy and importance.

With the Unit now fully manned, Stirling took his men to their first base set in desolate country at Kabrit, 100 miles from Cairo and lying on the edge of the Great Bitter Lake. The 'camp' comprised two sleeping tents, a supply tent and a truck. Furnishings were all but non-existent—one table and a couple of chairs. While Stirling had no intentions of cosseting his men, he did believe in providing at least the bare essentials, and these he did not have. It was, he realised, quite pointless requisitioning all the trappings via the normal channels; he would have to 'acquire' them by his own means.

Stirling knew of a New Zealand troop encampment not far from his own and, from all reports, it was well stocked with goodies. By comparison with the conditions under which his men were living, the Kiwis were enjoying unparalleled luxury, and this grated upon Stirling's sense of justice. 'Share and share alike' was his motto. So the SAS went on its first raid and the housing problem was solved overnight. With that difficulty removed, Stirling set his men to training with a vengeance. Discipline was strict and the training tough. Officers and men alike suffered the rigours of incredible physical punishment in a programme designed to bring them to the peak of fitness as quickly as possible. Although it was a gruelling experience, morale was high and they were all in fine spirits. They would be called upon to fight like tigers and Stirling whetted their appetites for the fray. Night after night groups of them set off on mock raids, putting into practice all the techniques of stealth they had been taught during the day in Stirling's desert classroom. They acquired the cunning of the hunter and the caution of the hunted. Each man became a marksman with a whole variety of weapons of all makes, British, Italian and German. So skilled did they become that they could strip them down and reassemble them blindfold. They became expert cut-throats, perfecting the art of silent killing with the knife. Night became their friend and they soon acquired the prowess of panthers.

The mock raids were 'fun' compared with the route marches they were forced to undertake both by day and night. In the burning heat of the day, men cursed and sweated under a cruel sun as they tramped across the desert. One stalwart, Private Lewis, epitomised the grit and determination Stirling instilled in his men when, on one particularly gruelling march, his boots disintegrated. Undaunted, he took them off and walked the remaining forty miles back to base in bare feet. And this he accomplished while carrying a pack of equipment weighing 75 pounds.

By night the men of the SAS froze on these marches, even though they were muffled in greatcoats. It was one of the phenomena of the desert. By day temperatures soared to more than one hundred degrees in the shade but at night they often dropped below freezing point.

Then came the parachute training, undertaken in aeroplanes

still not properly equipped for the duty. The first two drops were completed successfully but on the third, Stirling had the horrific experience of seeing two of his men fall to their deaths only yards from where he stood after their parachutes had failed to open. It appeared that the fault lay in the clips on the static lines attached to a rail in the aircraft. Tragic though this terrible accident was, there was little time to pause for emotion or sentiment. A new static line clip was substituted and the following day Stirling showed what he was made of when he insisted upon being the first to jump. Luckily, all went well and now, with the assistance of a newly-arrived parachute instructor the airborne training continued.

Landing by parachute was always a tricky business and to toughen up his men to this, Stirling devised a method of familiarising them with the hazard of landing in strong winds. To simulate such conditions, he had his men leaping off trucks racing across the desert at speeds of 30 mph and more, doing both forward and backward rolls.

As the days passed, L Detachment was groomed into a tough, disciplined band of raiders, itching to get into the scrap. Their first taste of a raid came about in a most unusual way—as the result of a bet.

Not everyone was convinced of the potential of the SAS desert raiders. In particular there was a certain RAF group captain who scoffed at the very idea that the SAS could penetrate an airfield, plant bombs on enemy aircraft then retreat unseen into the desert.

'All right then,' Stirling said, 'I'll bet you ten pounds that we can get into the airfield at Heliopolis, plant stickers on your aircraft then be gone without your sentries even knowing we've been. How about it?'

'You're on, old chap,' the flier said confidently. 'You've got yourself a wager.' As we have seen, the Group Captain lost his ten pounds.

Stirling's mock attack did much to convince the sceptics that the SAS would soon be a force to be reckoned with. If they could carry out a raid against an RAF airfield which was already alerted and get away with it, there was a damned good chance that they could do the same thing against an unprepared enemy.

There was however one serious problem to be overcome before any raid could take place. Stirling's raid against the airfield at

Heliopolis had been made easier by the fact that each man had only to carry a pocketful of stickers, a box of dates and some water. There was no doubt that things would be very much more difficult when they had to carry a load of bombs with them. The smallest type of portable bomb was much too heavy to be carried in any quantity. To be really effective it was vital that each of the raiders should be able to carry as many bombs as possible to do the maximum damage.

Furthermore, it was essential that they should find a bomb which was not only small and portable but both explosive and incendiary. This combination was crucial to ensure that the aircraft was both blown up and burned out so that the enemy could not salvage any of it after the attack. But when Stirling approached the explosives experts he was told that there was no such bomb available. 'Well,' he thought, 'if they haven't got one, we'll just have to make our own.'

He conferred with his officers and Jock Lewes volunteered to carry out some tests. He immediately set up shop and got down to business, experimenting with a whole variety of explosive substances. For days the desert around the camp reverberated to explosions, but try as he might, Lewes could not come up with the right combination. That is, until he tried an amalgam of plastic, thermite and oil which he mixed together and kneaded into a ball about the size of a tennis ball. He placed his bomb on top of an oil drum and inserted a fuse, then lit it and darted away. Seconds later there was a violent roar, the oil drum was ripped apart and the liquid inside blazed. He'd got it—a bomb which would not only tear an aircraft open but also transform it into a raging inferno.

Elated at his success, he told Stirling who promptly christened the new weapon, the Lewes Bomb. It was light, weighing about a pound, and devastatingly effective. A man could carry between twenty and thirty quite comfortably, which gave him a frightening destructive potential.

With the problem of the bomb overcome, the men of the SAS were ready for action. They did not have to wait long.

At this time General Auchinleck was planning his first major offensive against the Afrika Korps. This push was designed to relieve the beleaguered garrison of Tobruk which was under siege by Axis forces, then rout the Italian and German forces from

Cyreniaca. The offensive was to open at dawn on 18 November 1941, but its outcome depended in no small measure upon who ruled the air over the battle zone. The struggle for air superiority was a bitter and bloody one in the clear blue skies of the desert. Armoured columns were at the mercy of bomb-laden aircraft which could sweep down, raining bombs upon them. Air domination was crucial, and this was where Stirling was to play his part. If he could attack the main Axis airfields and blow up their aircraft on the ground, there would be fewer enemy aeroplanes in the sky to menace Auchinleck's army. It was therefore planned that the SAS would launch concerted attacks upon five of Rommel's airfields on the eve of the offensive.

For the first time Stirling could lead his men into action against the enemy. Among the men of the SAS, excitement grew to fever pitch in eager anticipation of the forthcoming raids.

On the 15th of that month the raiders boarded aircraft and were flown to a forward air base at Fuka where the final preparations for the raids got under way. Bombs, fuses, grenades, Tommy guns and all the other pieces of equipment vital to the raids were packed into special canisters which would be dropped by parachute with the men.

The target airfields lay in the Gazala-Tmimi area and it was planned that the raiders would be dropped by parachute on the night of the 16th, then hide up in the rocky escarpment nearby until the evening of the 17th when they would launch their attacks. When their job was done they would march forty-five miles into the desert to a prearranged rendezvous point, where they would meet up with a unit of the Long Range Desert Group which would take them back to their RAF base. The LRDG was a highly-specialised, mobile organisation whose primary function was that of a reconnaissance behind enemy lines. Their knowledge of the desert regions was unmatched by any other force. Operating the patrols, they scoured the desert in their trucks and kept a watchful eye on enemy troop movements. If anyone could get the SAS home safely, the LRDG could.

That was the plan. It was doomed to go tragically awry.

Stirling and his men waited throughout the day of the 16th with keen anticipation, cleaning weapons, sharpening their knives and keeping themselves generally active to allay pre-raid nerves. But as the day progressed a natural hazard threatened the whole raid.

The weather gradually worsened. A gale-force wind sprang up and Stirling was advised to cancel the raid. Parachuting at night was fraught with danger, even in the best conditions, but with a strong wind howling across the desert it was verging on the suicidal. Reports arrived indicating 90 mph gusts of wind near to the dropping zone. In these conditions there was an even greater danger of injuries and a certainty that the wind would blow them out of the dropping zone. Stirling was faced with a difficult decision. If he called off the raid, the doubters in Cairo would inevitably cry 'chicken' and if he went ahead with it and it failed, the SAS might well be disbanded as ineffective.

He called a conference and together, he and his officers weighed up the situation. The morale of his men was higher than ever. They had been trained to a physical and mental peak for this event and to deny it to them now would come as a bitter blow and might dampen their spirit for future operations. With the wisdom of a scholar Lewes observed, quite rightly, that in wartime conditions were rarely ideal for any attack and if they waited for perfect conditions, they would wait in vain and in all probability never get a crack at the enemy. That was it—the raid was on.

A little after 1700 hours, the raiders strode out to their waiting aircraft. They were Bristol Bombay transports—the best they could find. Ungainly twin-engined aeroplanes with a top speed of just under 200 miles an hour, they had been obsolete even before the war began but under the circumstances the SAS was lucky to get them.

There were five airfields to attack and the raiders were split up into five groups, each of which boarded a separate aircraft. The groups were led by Stirling, Lewes, McGonigal, Mayne and Bonnington each of whom was in charge of his own aircraft.

At 1930 hours, the airfield shook as all five aircraft roared into life and lifted into the darkening sky. Within them the men sat silent, deep in their own private thoughts. It was a cold, uncomfortable ride, with wind whistling through every tiny crevice in the aircraft's fuselage, adding to the discomfort of flying in an aircraft buffeted by the violent gusts of wind. To make matters worse the pilots were having difficulty navigating because the high winds had whipped up a sandstorm, making it impossible to pin-point landmarks on the ground.

Stirling was beginning to feel anxious about their chances of finding their targets, let alone jumping safely. The flight seemed to drag on for an eternity until suddenly, the aircraft lurched crazily as the pilot banked steeply. All around the aircraft the sky erupted as flak shells burst dangerously close to them. The sounds of the explosions reached the ears of the men huddled in the aircraft and did nothing to strengthen their nerves for the coming onslaught. Unaccustomed to attack in the air they felt vulnerable and out of their natural element. The heat of a battle on the ground was one thing and they could cope with that, but up here in the air was quite a different kettle of fish. The evasive action taken by the aircraft threw them wildly off course, so that they had great difficulty in finding the right track once more. Precious time was being lost in this cavorting about the sky until at last the warning lights lit inside the aircraft. They were only six minutes from the dropping zone—or so the pilots hoped.

In Stirling's aircraft, as in the others, an airman hauled open the door and the sudden inrush of air shook the numbed senses of the raiders. Each man tested his harness and clipped in to static lines. Standing one behind the other with Stirling in the lead, they waited for the green light. All eyes were fixed on it. The red warning light blinked, then went out. The green light shone and Stirling dropped out of the aircraft into the darkness, followed closely by the others.

Stirling felt a sudden jar as his canopy cracked open above his head, arresting his rapid descent and he floated peacefully towards the ground. He searched the dark sky above him for any sight of the others but saw none of them—nor could he see the ground when he glanced down beneath his feet. It seemed that he was falling into a bottomless, black void. He knew that the ground was there—but where? He braced himself for the landing that never seemed to come. Then it did—and he hit the desert with a crashing blow that knocked him unconscious. The blackout was only momentary but when he regained his senses he found himself being dragged along the ground. The strong wind had caught his open parachute. Automatically he twisted the release disc at his stomach and rapped it with a sharp blow. The harness fell away and the parachute shot off into the darkness, leaving Stirling alone and badly bruised from the impact of his landing.

Gathering his wits, Stirling looked around in a bid to find the others but they were nowhere to be seen. He flashed his torch into the night. There was no reply. It became more and more apparent as the minutes passed that the worst had happened. The violent wind had cast his men about the sky and scattered them over a wide area. It took Stirling almost an hour to round up most of his group. They were in a pitiful state, having suffered a similar fate to himself. Every single one was injured, some only slightly but others more seriously with broken limbs. Stirling could see with increasing clarity as he mustered his crippled band that their raid at least was doomed to failure. There was worse to come. Stirling took stock of the fighting equipment which had been parachuted down with them. The containers which were packed with bombs, fuses, machine guns, food and blankets were strewn across the desert. Only a handful of them could be found—and not nearly enough to carry out the raid with the remotest chance of success. It was hopeless and Stirling knew it. The first SAS raid was already a disastrous failure. He saw all the rugged training, all the careful planning crumble before his eyes. He was left with no alternative but to send his men limping off into the desert to rendezvous with the Long Range Desert Group.

But Stirling did not go with them. He resolved to salvage something of the operation. If he could not return with a claim of having destroyed enemy aircraft he could at least gather as much intelligence as possible whilst he was behind the lines. Stirling recruited Sergeant Tait to accompany him and the duo set off north to carry out a reconnaissance of the coast road to determine the volume of enemy traffic using it.

There was a long trek ahead of them to the road and as they plodded on, a cloudburst brought a torrent of rain upon them. Within minutes they were drenched and uncomfortable. Rainwater trickled down the backs of their necks and coursed over their sweating skin. Visibility was severely limited in the blur of the rain as it poured down on them. What had been firm, rock-strewn ground was quickly transformed into a squelching morass. The *wadis* through which they had to pass to reach the road became raging torrents of water and they were forced to wade waist-deep into them. As they battled their way on into the storm, the weather grew progressively worse. Driving rain lashed their faces, biting and stinging like a thousand needles.

Each step became an agony, taxing their waning strength. They still had a great distance to cover before coming to the road and

Stirling realised that even if they did reach it, a proper reconnaissance would now be impossible in the blinding rain. Dejected, Stirling and Tait turned and retraced their steps to head for the rendezvous point.

When they finally reached the rendezvous with the LRDG they found the men having a brew-up. The steaming hot tea restored some vestige of life to them and with his spirits gradually rising, Stirling had a look around his men. Of the sixty who had set out on the raids, only twenty-two had returned. Fraser and Lewes had arrived safely, but had lost some of their men. It was not until morning that Paddy Mayne got back with his nine men.

Stirling waited all day and into the following night, hoping that the others might struggle in, but they did not come. The awful truth had to be faced. They were not coming. They had been either killed or captured.

It was not until very much later that Stirling discovered what had become of Bonnington and his men. Bonnington's aircraft, piloted by Warrant Officer Charles West, was subjected to the same appalling weather conditions encountered by the others. Blinding sandstorms, lightning and torrential rain summoned their combined natural strength to cast the Bombay far off course. West and his crew struggled to regain the proper track and in a bid to do this the pilot took the Bombay low to duck under the cloud base and determine his position by sighting landmarks. Almost skimming across the desert, West's Bombay flew into the teeth of an intense barrage of anti-aircraft fire. Shells and machinegun fire raked the aircraft, putting the port engine out of action and peppering the length of the fuselage with holes. The instrument panel fell victim to a spray of bullets which tore it apart. Without it, navigation in cloud was all but impossible.

The wing petrol tanks were punctured by bullets and precious fuel streamed out of them. The fuel gauges trembled and fell as the tanks spewed out their load at an alarming rate until finally they registered empty. West now had no alternative but to land. Amid hellish weather he selected a darkened strip of desert and prayed that there were no obstacles in his path. Then he put the aircraft down. Luck was with him for, despite a few bumps, the aircraft touched down without sustaining further damage.

Just before dawn, Bonnington led a patrol out into the desert in a bid to discover exactly where they were. Of one thing there was

and a few mud huts but apart from these the oasis was a deserted sandy waste infested by flies. Despite these drawbacks, Stirling found the new base ideal for his purposes.

The oasis was already occupied by British forces, having been captured from the Italians only a short time before. The garrison was commanded by Brigadier Reid, a tough, courageous soldier. There was a critical shortage of supplies but Reid welcomed Stirling with open arms, offering him all the help he could give. In his new home Stirling felt that at last he could hit the enemy hard. He had not long to wait before an opportunity presented itself.

One day towards the end of November 1941, Reid came to Stirling and announced that he had been ordered to leave Jalo and head north-west to link up with Brigadier Marriot. The object of the move was to ensnare Rommel as he retreated towards Benghazi. But there were problems. During the move across the desert, Reid's columns would be exposed to attack from the air by the Luftwaffe. The result could be disaster. There was only one way of ensuring a safe transit and that was to destroy as many as possible of the enemy aircraft, especially fighters, before they could take off. The greatest threat of attack came from Agedabia and Reid asked Stirling if he could mount a raid upon that and other airfields the night before he was to make his move. Stirling relished the prospect and agreed at once.

After he had begun planning the raid, Stirling decided which of the other enemy airfields to attack. He, along with Paddy Mayne and a small group would strike the airfield at Sirte, 350 miles from Jalo, while Jock Lewes, leading another group, would attack the airfield at El Agheila. The third raid was to be led by Bill Fraser who would attack the field at Agedabia, the closest airfield to Benghazi. If they could pull off these raids on the same night, 14th December, the result would be a crippling blow to the Axis air strength.

Because of the varying distances from Jalo to the target airfields, the parties were to leave Jalo at different times so that they could launch their attacks simultaneously on the 14th.

Travel across the desert was fraught with hazards, not the least of which were the razor-sharp rocks strewn over much of the ground. These tore tyres and caused many punctures, making regular wheel changes a necessity. The men of the LRDG were experts in desert travel and knew the difficulties they would be facing so it was decided that Stirling's party, which had farthest to go, would leave Jalo on 8th December, giving them ample time to reach the target.

On the appointed departure date, all was ready for the off. The camouflaged 30-cwt. trucks, painted a bright rose colour which made them almost invisible from the air, were loaded with all the goods that were needed for the journey and the raid: spare tyres, ammunition, weapons, petrol cans, blankets, food; not to mention the huge camouflage nets which were a vital part of their equipment when they were threatened with air attack. The trucks were piled so high with supplies that the thirty-two officers and men of the SAS and LRDG barely had room to sit and had to find convenient niches wherever they could amid the bundles.

After a final check of the equipment, the trucks set off from Jalo with Gus Holliman, the LRDG commander, and Mike Sadler, the navigator, in the lead truck and Stirling in the vehicle behind. The other five trucks carried the remainder of the party. As they struck out across the barren desert the sun rose higher in the sky and reached an intensity that seemed to burn into their brains. There was no shade from the heat, and they had to strip off their clothes, leaving their bodies exposed to the sun's burning rays.

That first day passed without incident and they made good time on their journey. When darkness came they made camp and got down to the tiresome but vital business of servicing their vehicles and cleaning their weapons. Meanwhile the radio operator tuned into LRDG headquarters to get up-to-date news of the progress of the war. Night brought with it bitter cold which made sleep difficult and they were weary when they finally awoke.

They set off again across the desert and the only obstacles that impeded their progress were the inevitable delays to change tyres after punctures. To do this it was necessary to unload all the equipment from a truck before jacking it up to change the tyre. After doing this several times in the sweltering heat of the desert, tempers were inclined to become frayed, but in spite of these frustrating set-backs the men continued to make fairly good speed all that day and throughout the one that followed.

On their fourth day out, however, they encountered their first real trouble when one of the men spotted an Italian Gibli reconnaissance aircraft flying towards them. As soon as the alarm was raised the gunners leapt to their Lewis guns mounted on each of the trucks. When the Gibli came within range they opened fire, sending up a barrage of fire at the swooping aircraft.

The Italian dived down on the column and unleashed two bombs which whistled through the air and exploded well off target. Then the Gibli banked sharply away and soon was only a tiny speck far off in the dazzling sky. The gunners had failed to find their mark and Stirling knew that it would only be a matter of time before the enemy came out after them in strength. Quickly they wheeled the trucks round and dashed for a patch of scrub. The bushes and rocks afforded little or no cover for the trucks but at least the men could crouch behind them. Wasting no time they covered the trucks with the camouflage nets and scurried into whatever cover they could find. Then they waited for the inevitable drone of aircraft engines. They were soon heard . . .

Stirling and Holliman lay together in the sand and watched as three Italian bombers appeared in the sky, the pilots scouring the desert for the trucks. The aircraft flew low and then they must have caught sight of the wheel tracks that ran into the camouflaged humps, for seconds later the bombs began to fall. They hurtled towards the sand and exploded with a *crump* while the Italian gunners raked the sand with machine-gun fire. The men on the ground could do nothing but lie motionless and pray that their names would not be on these bombs. For almost a quarter of an hour the aircraft saturated the area with bombs. Then they re-grouped and flew off. It was over.

Stirling hauled himself to his feet and brushed the sand off his clothes. To his amazement he saw that not one of the trucks had been hit and no one was injured. It was incredible, considering the intensity of the attack and the men could not believe their remarkable escape. The decision was made to celebrate with lunch.

After their meal they started off once more but later, when the light was beginning to fade, they had another close shave when the Gibli flew high above them again, then turned away. They had clearly been seen but Holliman reckoned that the Italians would not send bombers out to attack them during the hours of darkness. He was right.

By then they were only a few miles from their target, the airfield at Sirte, and soon it was dark. They were forced to continue throughout the night, without lights, which made negotiating the rugged desert extremely difficult. Nosing their way through the night, they suddenly heard voices and the sound of revving engines. The horrible truth quickly dawned—they were only yards away from the coast road, which was still in enemy hands.

Discovery at that time might have ruined the entire mission and Stirling did not want a recurrence of what had happened previously. It was clear that the Italians were patrolling the coast road, hunting for the column the Gibli had spotted earlier. Talking in whispers, Stirling outlined a hastily contrived alternative plan. Now that the Italians knew they were in the area the SAS might have to fight it out, so he decided that the best chance of success lay in splitting into two groups. Stirling and Sergeant Brough would attack Sirte airfield and Paddy Mayne would take a group of men and attack a newly-built airfield near the town of Tamit.

Stirling and Sergeant Brough would set off and hide near to the airfield the following day until the time came to attack Sirte. It was arranged that the LRDG would pick them up immediately after at a point near the coast road. Now that all the arrangements had been made, Stirling and Brough made off into the night, carrying their bombs and weapons, while the LRDG trucks headed toward Tamit to drop off Mayne and his group.

The two men scrambled into the darkness, searching for a place to hide out for the day and if possible get a good view of the airfield. They stumbled on over the rock-strewn sand until a shadow loomed large in front of them. They crept nearer—it was a parked aircraft. They had walked on to the airfield!

Stirling had expected to find at least a fence or some sort of barbed wire entanglement around the airfield but the Italians had obviously not taken the precaution of laying one. The two men could hardly believe that they had been able to walk on to the airfield without even a challenge—but there they were.

Stirling whispered to Brough that they were to make a reconnaissance and they gingerly edged farther on to the field. They discovered more and more aircraft parked in a long line, apparently without any guard on them. The temptation to plant their bombs there and then was great but Stirling knew only too well that if he did so he might ruin Paddy Mayne's chances of pulling off his attack. The element of surprise would be gone for Paddy when the hornet's nest was roused and the success of a raid depended almost entirely upon that crucial element. So Stirling had no choice but to temper his desire to bomb them.

They slipped away from the parked aircraft and were heading away from the airfield when suddenly Stirling's foot caught something on the ground. That 'something' was an Italian sentry *asleep* on the ground. A frightened yell echoed across the silent airfield. Stirling and Brough broke into a run and bolted into the darkness of the desert, closely followed by a hail of bullets that zipped through the air around them.

They dashed farther on until the ground shook as heavy anti-aircraft guns opened up. But the guns were not firing in their direction—they were aimed out to sea. The Italians mistakenly thought that they were being attacked by commandos coming at them from the sea. This suited Stirling perfectly and he and Brough made for a nearby ridge where they took cover. After a while the noise died and silence returned to the area. Both men settled down to sleep. Lying amid some scrub which offered good cover, they slept peacefully for the remainder of the night.

When dawn came they found they had a perfect view of the airfield. They watched as bombers took-off and landed and Stirling's eyes glinted at the prospect of the coming night's raid. There were always thirty aircraft at least on the field at one time. The loss of these thirty Caprioni would severely cripple the Axis war effort and Stirling couldn't wait for the night and the chance to have a crack at them. But in the meantime the two of them had to conserve their energies for the night's work, so they decided to have some more sleep. Again they lapsed into sleep, only to be awakened with a start. They could hear the sound of voices. Only a few yards from where they lay was a group of Arabs working on a plot of cultivated land. Of all the places they could have picked they had to choose this one.

If the Arabs discovered them there was little doubt that that would be the end of the raid. The two SAS men lay motionless, hardly daring to breathe, until at last the Arabs left. The two men sighed and turned their heads once more to the airfield. But another shock was in store for them. Throughout the afternoon, bombers took off in pairs—and did not return. By dusk, the airfield was deserted. Stirling realised that the airfield had been evacuated. All his targets—thirty Caprioni bombers—were gone. He was furious. To have come this far only to suffer the frustration of watching his targets slips away from him was just too much. He cursed his luck and, bitterly disappointed, settled down to wait until it was time to set out and rendezvous with the LRDG.

Only one thought gave heart to the dejected Stirling and that was the possibility that Paddy Mayne might meet with success. As darkness overtook the desert he gloomily pondered upon the thought that if Paddy's raid was a failure, the SAS would undoubtedly be disbanded. Two failures in a row was too much for any high command to tolerate.

After dark, Stirling and Brough left their hiding place and headed for the coast road to meet up with the LRDG.

It was a little after 2200 hours when they reached the road. Both men lay there anxiously peering into the night in the direction of Paddy's airfield. They hoped to see flashes as his bombs blew up and signalled his success, but the appointed hour of the attack came and went. All was still on the horizon. It seemed that Stirling's worst fears were to be realised as the agony of waiting continued. He need not have worried. The redoutable Paddy Mayne and his band of raiders had been delayed but were now embarking upon their attack.

The airfield at Tamit lay in silent darkness as Mayne led his men in single file across the perimeter. Bomb-laden and with Tommy guns ready they stole forward, their eyes searching the night for sentries. None were visible and they continued towards a cluster of buildings.

Moving now with ghostlike swiftness they darted to the wall of a building. At the foot of a door, Mayne saw a thin ribbon of light. From behind that door came the sound of laughter and the excited and gay chatter of Italians. It sounded as if there was a celebration of some sort in full swing and Mayne resolved to crash the party. He darted to the door, cocking his Tommy gun as he went. Then he paused, only for a moment, his hand on the door handle. He twisted it, pushed and fired without waiting to see what was inside. The muzzle of the Tommy gun waved to and fro as Mayne sprayed the room with bullets, and the Italians caught the full blast. The carousing revellers slumped and fell as the missiles thudded into their bodies. What had been a scene of merriment was transformed in an instant into a bloody massacre. Mayne lifted the Tommy gun and sprayed the lights, plunging the room into darkness. Then he slammed the door shut and ran. Within the room the floor was strewn with dead and dying men. Moans and screams of agony now replaced the laughter that had filled it only minutes before.

The dazed Italians who had escaped Mayne's onslaught pulled pistols from their holsters and stumbled to the windows to fire blindly into the night. Still running, Mayne yelled to his men to keep the Italians penned in while he led the others to the dark shapes of the aircraft on the far side of the airfield.

He and five others darted from plane to plane planting their bombs with practised skill. They knew just where to put them to effect the greatest damage. Then they reached the last aeroplane, only to find that they were one bomb short—but this was not to deter the Ulsterman. Mayne clambered into the cockpit and with his bare hands ripped out the control and instrument panel. Then he leapt from the aeroplane and bawled to the others to make a dash for the desert.

As they grouped up and ran off into the night, the ground shook when the first of the bombs exploded. A bomber was enveloped in a great ball of flame. A split second later, another was engulfed in fire. Vast tongues of flame leapt into the air as more and more aircraft were embraced in the volcanic grip of the holocaust. Then it seemed as if the world was afire when a petrol dump blew up.

The fleeing raiders paused for only a few seconds to glance back at the results of their handiwork. The entire field seemed to be ablaze. Against the backcloth of searing flame, they could see enraged Italians darting about in a hopeless attempt to find them while others made a vain attempt to douse the inferno.

Racing blindly on into the darkness of the desert and leaving the blazing firework display behind them, Mayne and his men lost their way but luckily the LRDG was near at hand and they met up with them after a series of blasts on their whistles. The raiders were beside themselves with joy at the success of the night's work and it was in this jubilant mood that they scrambled aboard the trucks and bumped off into the night.

Meanwhile, far off by the coast road, Stirling had witnessed the most welcome of sights. On the horizon he saw the red glow from the burning and exploding aircraft. Thanks to Paddy Mayne, the SAS was saved.

Just as the red glow was fading from the sky, the LRDG arrived to pick up Stirling and Brough and they headed for their desert rendezvous with Paddy Mayne. When they eventually met deep in the desert, Stirling learned that Mayne had destroyed no fewer than twenty-four aircraft. At last the SAS had struck a crushing blow at the enemy. In high spirits they headed back for their base at Jalo.

Stirling's thoughts were with the other groups—Jock Lewes's which had attacked El Agheila, and Bill Fraser's which had gone for Agedabia.

Lewes was the first to return, and he had been unlucky. He had discovered that the airfield was no more than a ferrying point. But his raid had not been altogether fruitless. Intelligence he had gleaned before leaving Jalo had indicated that there was, quite near the airfield, a roadhouse which was frequented by high-ranking officers of the Axis forces. Determined not to leave without making his mark, Lewes decided to launch an attack upon it.

It so happened that the truck in which he was travelling was a captured Italian Lancia and although it carried British markings, Lewes thought it might be just the thing to pull off a daring piece of deception and get him and his men close enough to raid the roadhouse.

The Lancia lay in hiding by the coastal roadside and waited until a convoy of Italian lorries came along. When the last one had passed, the bold Lewis and his band of saboteurs drove out of hiding and tagged on to the end of the stream of vehicles. All went well for a while until the blatant British markings were spotted just as they were nearing the roadhouse. The result was a battle royal with enemy guns trained on the Lancia.

The quick-thinking Lewes divided his men into two groups, one to keep up the battle with the Italians and the other to carry out a raid on an enemy transport park nearby. While the battle raged in the background, Lewes and a handful of others planted bombs on as many trucks as they could find. The short fuses burned out and in an instant the entire transport park was wiped out, leaving nothing but smouldering wrecks. In the confusion that ensued, Lewes and his band made their escape.

When Fraser returned four days later, he brought with him the most spectacular news of all. He and his group had blown up thirty-seven aircraft. In fact, as he revealed, the aircraft had begun to blow up before they had planted all their bombs. He was forced to leave two aircraft undamaged through lack of explosives. Luckily the chaos resulting from the explosions gave them the break they needed to make their escape from the field. All this he achieved with the aid of just three men.

With a score of 'kills' for the night of sixty-one aircraft totally destroyed and a healthy number of transports wrecked, Stirling had good cause to feel that the future of the SAS was secure. He and his men had proved beyond doubt that they had a force to be reckoned with. In that night they had knocked out more aircraft than any single RAF fighter pilot could lay claim to in the entire war—and they were by no means finished.

Stirling was eager and restless to keep hitting the enemy. Replacement aircraft for those blown up by the SAS were ferried into North Africa, only to be attacked and blown up before they could get into action. The raids were stepped up and the number of destroyed enemy aircraft rocketed.

Night after night Stirling launched raids, emerging out of the dark, swooping down on airfields then fading into the night once more, leaving destruction in his wake. Axis sentries became edgy and nervous of the night, never knowing when their turn might come. Morale amongst the enemy slumped.

But these raids were not carried out without cost to the SAS. Tragedy struck when Jock Lewes mounted a raid on an enemy airfield. He had succeeded in destroying just one aircraft and when he and his men were making their escape back across the desert, they came under attack from the air. Lewes was hit and died within minutes. The SAS had lost one of its finest officers. In yet another raid, the detachment almost lost its leader too . . .

The incident occurred one night when Stirling was leading a party of his men on an attack. On his way to carry out the raid his path was blocked by a heavy enemy armoured column. Stirling had no alternative but to abandon his raid and return to the rendezvous point with the LRDG. But when he met up with them in the night, he forgot the password. He was challenged by a sentry. The sentry fired at Stirling but by some miracle, his weapon misfired and the architect of the SAS was spared.

There were other moments of high tension, like the one that befell Sergeant Phillips who found himself stranded in the desert. An enemy truck came trundling in his direction so the wily sergeant pulled a blanket over his head, disguising himself as an

Arab. Waving his arms in the air he brought the truck to a halt. It had no sooner stopped than Phillips tossed aside the blanket and fired at the occupants of the truck, killing them all. Then he disposed of the corpses and commandeered the truck which he used to return to his unit.

Phillips was luckier than some of his comrades. After an abortive attack on an Italian airfield, Fraser and his men missed their rendezvous with the LRDG. They waited patiently in the desert for six days until finally their water supply ran out. Two hundred miles lay between them and their base—so Fraser decided to walk it. *Eight days later*, almost driven mad by thirst and fatigue, they stumbled into their base.

In the meantime, Stirling kept up his raids, not restricting them to airfields. He blew up fuel dumps, wiped out dozens of German transport trucks in one swift attack, mined roads and even attacked German armoured columns on the main coastal route.

David Stirling was a man who continuously sought new ways of hitting at the enemy, perfecting the technique of clandestine confusion and destruction. Experience had shown him that he and his men were highly vulnerable to capture immediately after a raid if they did not escape quickly and he pondered upon how to overcome this. He hit on the idea of using jeeps suitably armed with machine guns which could dash on to an airfield, shoot up the aircraft and race off into the night before the enemy could collect his wits.

The more he considered the idea, the more appealing it became and he lost no time in acquiring a fleet of brand new jeeps. They were fitted with four Lewis guns, one pair mounted in front in the passenger's seat and another pair at the back of the jeep. Stirling planned that each jeep would carry a crew of three, comprising a driver and two gunners.

Now that he had the jeeps Stirling was determined to put them to work. The German airfield at Sidi Haneish, near Fuka, was the target. He would use eighteen jeeps but before embarking upon the raid he wisely decided to have a full dress rehearsal in the desert. It was as well that he did for it soon became clear that this type of attack had one major hazard—and that was for the drivers of the jeeps.

They set off into the desert travelling in two columns about six yards apart with Stirling's jeep in the lead. At a signal from

Stirling, the jeeps fanned out into a V formation. The gunners in the right-hand column fired at imaginary aircraft on the right, while the gunners in the left-hand column fired at 'aircraft' on the left. All the jeeps were left-hand drive and as a result the unfortunate drivers in the left-hand column found themselves with bullets whipping past their heads from the guns in the passenger seats. It meant in effect that a driver dared not move his head forward more than a couple of inches or it would be blown off. As the jeeps were travelling over rock strewn terrain, this was no easy task. Despite this the practice run went smoothly and all that remained was for them to make the final preparations for the raid proper.

A last-minute reconnaissance of the target airfield revealed that there was always a large number of aircraft on the field at any one time, mostly Junkers JU 52 troop transports, a type of aircraft which Rommel could ill afford to lose, since they were in critically short supply in the desert. Stirling aimed to add to Rommel's difficulty by subtracting them from his strength.

Just before dusk on 26 July, the jeeps assembled and a final check was carried out before they set out into the desert for the 40-mile journey to Sidi Haneish. They drove off into the growing darkness, winding their way across the difficult terrain and keeping up a reasonable speed of around twenty miles an hour.

The burden of navigation lay squarely upon the shoulders of Mike Sadler. He had already proved his exceptional skill in desert navigation on many raids before, delivering the raiders to their exact destinations under the most impossible conditions. The success of this raid depended very largely upon his skill. If he miscalculated and they even narrowly missed the airfield and had to manoeuvre to find it, then the element of surprise would be lost and the raid would fail. After they had gone some way, Sadler stopped and erected his theodolite to check their position. He seemed satisfied and they got underway once more.

As they bumped over the desert, the jeeps were slowed down by the menace that had dogged them so often in the past—punctures. By then, of course, they were experts in changing wheels, but nevertheless these tiresome stops added to the pre-raid tension.

The moon rose into the night sky as they drove on towards their target and the light cast up ghostly shadows around them.

Then a yell came from one of the jeeps. Ahead of the column one of the men had spotted a large black shape. Cautiously they nosed forward to find that the shape was a burnt out vehicle mangled into a grotesque shape by shell fire. They soon discovered that more wrecked vehicles were strewn around them. There had been a battle in the area not long before and this was the graveyard for these fighting vehicles. Stirling had had reports of a battle not far from Sidi Haneish and he knew therefore that they were not far from their goal, probably only about a mile. Now was the time to get into their proper formations and the jeeps manoeuvred into two neat columns of eight with Stirling's jeep at front in the centre and Sadler's in the middle at the rear.

The jeeps nosed forward as the moon slipped behind the cloud. In the darkness Stirling could see nothing of the airfield. Then suddenly the whole desert was bathed in light. There in front of them, barely half a mile away was the airfield with all its lights on.

Instantly Stirling thought the game was up and that they had been discovered. The enemy must have got wind of them and were waiting but his fears were quickly dispelled when the dull roar of a bomber's engines reached their ears. It was coming in to land and the landing lights had been switched on for it.

Stirling did not hesitate and dashed forward with the other jeeps streaming behind him. They charged towards the field as the gunners cocked their guns. With only a hundred yards to go, Stirling opened up with his machine gun and all the others did likewise. In an instant the whole airfield reverberated to the sound of machine gun fire and tracer bullets.

In the lead jeep, Stirling fired a green Very light and the jeeps fanned out into V formation, wheeling on to the runway between two neat lines of parked aircraft. As the jeeps swept past the aircraft, the gunners sprayed them with bullets, ripping and tearing into the machines and igniting petrol tanks. One by one the planes glowed red then burst into flame and exploded in great sheaths of fire.

Junkers, Heinkels and Stuka dive bombers fell to the guns as the raiders riddled them with incendiary bullets. Sixty-eight machine guns firing 1,200 rounds a minute continued to pour lead into the parked machines but by then the Germans had come to life and were dashing for their defence posts, manning machineguns and mortars.

With a flash a mortar bomb landed in between the two columns of jeeps and exploded with a muffled crump but failed to do any damage.

Then a Breda cannon opened up on the jeeps and one of the raiders Steve Hastings felt something hot pass beneath his seat, followed instantly by a resounding clang. Immediately he and his driver were covered from head to toe in oil but the jeep continued on its way.

Just then Stirling's jeep was riddled with bullets and slowed to a halt. He and the other two men leapt off the jeep and were picked up by another. Stirling ordered the gunners to concentrate on the Breda cannon and machineguns swung to focus on it. In a split second it was silenced. By now the column was at a standstill and Stirling yelled fresh orders to the drivers telling them to circle the field and deal with remaining aircraft which had not yet been destroyed. The heat from the already blazing machines was intense and the jeeps moved off to find fresh targets.

They roared in amongst the planes once more and unleashed a concentrated hail of fire into them. The last of the aircraft seemed to refuse to catch light so Paddy Mayne leapt off his jeep and planted a bomb on it. Soon it too erupted in flame as the jeeps broke off their attack and roared off into the desert.

As they charged into the darkness, leaving behind them an airfield strewn with burning aircraft and a scene of utter devastation, Steve Hastings' jeep seized up. A bomb was quickly planted in it and it blew up.

Of the eighteen jeeps which had taken part in the raid, only fifteen remained and all but one of the raiders had escaped. The sole casualty was a front gunner who had been killed by shrapnel from a mortar bomb.

The jeeps split up and raced off into the night, driving until first light. Stirling knew that the Germans would send out what aircraft they could muster from other airfields to track down and attack them. Sure enough, when dawn came, the desert shook to the drone of Stuka dive bombers as they scoured the area for the SAS. One of the groups of jeeps was found and bombed and one man was killed. The remainder escaped to find their way back to base.

Stirling had an opportunity of counting the cost. Two men had been killed but the SAS had destroyed every aircraft on the airfield. The night's work had been highly successful. The first jeep raid was over, and had added yet more aircraft to their score of kills.

Led by the indomitable Stirling the SAS carried out more attacks, not only on airfields but on every conceivable kind of target, including enemy ships at anchor in harbours, oil pipe lines, enemy transports and many more. Stirling became one of the most wanted men in the desert, earning the nickname of the 'Phantom Major', but this did not deter him from carrying on the fight behind the enemy lines. The SAS caused so much damage that the Germans set up a special regiment to combat them. It was a unit of this regiment that finally caught up with Stirling. While he was having a brief sleep in a desert cave they found him and took him into captivity. He made four escape attempts, only to be recaptured and eventually confined in the notorious Colditz Castle where he remained until the end of the war.

With Stirling gone, Paddy Mayne took over command of the SAS, leading many more raids. When the war in the desert was over, he moved on to Europe. He soon earned the distinction of being the man who had destroyed more enemy aircraft with his own hands than any other alive. He also became the most decorated soldier in the British Army, with the DSO and three bars.

As for David Stirling, the brilliant and daring young Scot who had conceived the idea of the SAS and fought so hard to bring it to reality, he was admitted to the Distinguished Service Order. It hardly seems a fitting reward for the man whom Rommel described in his diary as 'the very able and adaptable commander of the desert group which had caused us more damage than any other British unit of equal strength.' Even Hitler admitted that 'These men are very dangerous' and ordered that they were to be hunted down and destroyed at all cost.

During the fourteen months for which Stirling commanded the Special Air Service, it was responsible for the destruction of no fewer than 250 enemy aircraft with very little loss to itself. The part it played in the North African campaign helped tilt the balance in favour of the British Army.

Stirling left the Army when the Second World War ended with the rank of colonel, leaving behind a regiment whose activities even today are shrouded in secrecy.

2

Shepherds of the Invasion

The first light of a wet, grey dawn illumined the waters off the Normandy coast of France. Upon the battlements of Hitler's European fortress, jack-booted troops in the murky green uniforms of the *Wehrmacht* yawned and stretched after their night-long vigil standing sentinel over German-occupied France. The beach at their feet and the sea of the English Channel that lapped against it were a common, invariably uninterrupted sight for them. Some cast a casual glance out into the early morning drizzle that veiled the Channel in a bid to determine what the weather might be on the coming day. But the casual glance detected something strange out there, something unusual. The haze-shrouded horizon was punctuated by indistinguishable dots . . . dots that were gradually taking shape, the shape of ships, not just one or two, not tens or even hundreds of them, but thousands. *Almost five thousand.* Aboard these boats and ships of all shapes and sizes were some two hundred thousand soldiers, sailors and marines. The greatest armada ever to be assembled in the history of mankind was amassing. . . .

It was June 6, 1944 and throughout the previous night this mighty force of ships had navigated its way from ports and anchorages along the length of southern England across the English Channel to the assembly points off the French coast. There they were poised before five invasion beaches. Following furious bombardments of the immediate shore defences, hundreds of landing craft swept ashore to disgorge several thousand assault troops. The bloody battles to gain a foothold in France had begun. It was the beginning of the end for the Third Reich.

But the troop-laden landing craft were not the first vessels to test the defences of the Normandy beaches. Lying a little way off the shore were two midget submarines which, like sea-borne traffic signs, directed the landing craft towards their beaches. Without them, chaos might well have reigned. The crews of these mini-subs belonged to a small, select and highly-secret unit known as Combined Operations Pilotage Parties. Long before the Normandy Invasion took place, the COPP had visited these shores and carried out searching reconnaissance missions, scouting the beaches under the very noses of the Germans. The lives of the invading troops depended in no small measure upon the accuracy of these reconnaissance missions, for it was known that there lay beneath the water's surface myriad obstacles, planted to foil an invasion. These had to be detected and if possible neutralised. Without such preparations, the carefully planned invasion might well have resulted in catastrophic loss of life, for the landing itself was far and away the most crucial stage in the operation. If it faltered on unforeseen obstacles, the invaders would be at the mercy of the defenders' guns. As it was, the invasion was a success, very largely because of the work done by the Combined Operations Pilotage Parties.

Unlike many of the innovations employed during the invasion, there was nothing new about COPP. It had been conceived in the mind of an energetic young naval officer, Lieutenant Commander Nigel Willmott who, despite the most incredible lack of foresight among some of his senior officers, gave birth to and commanded this small unit which was to play such a vital part in almost every major British invasion of the war.

Willmott, a career naval officer, was a specialist in the art of navigation whose peerless knowledge of charts and the skills of persuading a craft across seas where the only signposts were the stars and a compass, made him one of the Royal Navy's élite. Slim, grey-eyed, with angular features, he had about him an air of intensity. Some thought him remote, constantly pensive, detached, and religious. He was the antithesis of the gay young officer and even shunned popularity. He drank little and was that rare combination of intellectual and man of action. He appeared to prefer his own company to that of others. But these traits, seen by some as anti-social, were the hallmark of a man dedicated and absorbed in his job, whose mind seldom strayed from the testing task given him. This dedication was to prove a priceless asset to the Allies in the reclamation of Europe.

Early in the war, Willmott had witnessed the demise of many

British ships during the abortive Narvik campaign, that bitter battle fought during the fall of Norway. The staggering fact was that, of all the Royal Navy ships lost, half came to grief upon rocks or underwater shoals and not as a result of German fire-power. This had been caused through lack of knowledge of these waters brought about by inadequate and inaccurate charts. The unreliability of these charts was perhaps understandable, since their intention was to keep ships and boats away from danger *areas* and each underwater hazard was not marked individually in detail.

Following the catastrophe of Narvik Willmott began to apply his mind to the question of how to avoid a repetition of that debacle. The answer he arrived at was to be both dramatic and dangerous in the extreme. But it was to be some time before he was to be called upon to put it into practice.

1941 found Willmott in Cairo, far away from the icy fjords of Norway. The British and Commonwealth troops who thronged the streets of the ancient Egyptian city were in buoyant mood. General Wavell had all but routed an inferior Italian army and the bulk of it was embraced within the thonged grip of barbed wire. Three hundred thousand bewildered, shocked and in many cases relieved Italians had been captured. The victory had come as a welcome boost to the morale of the Allies and helped wrest them from the depression of the defeat they had suffered in Europe. The British and Commonwealth armies were in offensive mood and the war lords scanned the map for a target on which to inflict the victorious spirit of their forces. They chose the Italian-held island of Rhodes. From its airfields, Italian bombers were carrying out mine-laying operations in a bid to impede the passage of Allied ships in the Mediterranean. It also provided an ideal staging post for German aircraft en route for the Western Desert where they were beginning to make their presence felt by carrying out strafing attacks on Allied convoys. Rhodes had to be captured and an amphibious landing was planned. Nigel Willmott was appointed Navigator to the invasion force that was to launch the attack.

Willmott's most immediate task was to reconnoitre the coast of Rhodes and select the beaches best suited to the landings. A submarine was duly commandeered and with Willmott on board she crept into the shallows off the island. At the periscope, Willmott scanned the coastline as the submarine followed its contours. He was staggered at the great detail the powerful lenses showed him. Some enemy soldiers were clearly visible pacing their beat on sentry duty while others lounged around taking the sun. At five-minute intervals Willmott took snap looks at Rhodes, comparing the coastline as he saw it with the official chart. Finally the observation from the submarine was complete. Willmott's verdict: a pleasant day's sightseeing, but as a preparation for an invasion, a waste of time.

When he returned to Cairo and reviewed what he had discovered, he found to his horror that the charts he had compiled from the periscope survey were at one point a *mile* out. He was thunderstruck. A vision came to him of a fleet of troop- and tank-carrying craft 'hitting the beach' wildly off course, at positions totally unsuited to landings. He foresaw the invading force sailing into a concentration of enemy defences or, equally fatal, running aground on rocks, leaving themselves high and dry for enemy gunners to slaughter. Perfunctory peeps through a periscope were just not enough to give an attacking force a fair chance of getting ashore at the right place without falling foul of natural and enemy-built hazards.

The periscope reconnaissance had, however, not been altogether fruitless. Willmott had been able to pin-point some of the obvious enemy gun emplacements and at least rule out some landing points. He had earmarked others as 'possibles' but although they looked promising through the lens of a periscope and at least outwardly had all the attributes of good assault points, Willmott was far from pleased. The onus of landing the invasion force on suitable beaches lay squarely upon his shoulders. Willmott was more pensive than ever and he paced his room in Cairo with furrowed brow. How could he be sure that the beaches he chose for the landings were free of off-shore underwater reefs that weren't marked on the charts, or that the beach itself was not mined. Dreams of a disastrous debacle haunted him. He would wake up in the middle of the night bathed in cold sweat. He saw inexperienced landing craft commanders launched from their parent ships miles off shore unable to navigate their way to the proper beach. The nightmare spectre of a long coastline strewn with wrecked landing craft haunted him. He saw the bloated bodies of British soldiers floating faces down in the sea, thrust against the rocks with the force of the waves, an army slaughtered—and the fault was his.

Willmott cocooned himself in thought, searching for the answer. He remembered the story of how, in the First World War, prior to the Gallipoli landings, an officer had swum ashore and lit a beacon to guide in the invading ships. This recollection sparked off the germ of an idea that brought him to a firm decision. He determined to go ashore himself and carry out a systematic reconnaissance, not only of the beach, but of the waters immediately off it. These were the danger areas and Willmott became resolute in the thought that the landing force would not come to grief there on his account.

He jotted his ideas down on paper and as he did so it became increasingly apparent just how difficult and dangerous such an exploit would be. To be sure of the water's depth off-shore he would have to take soundings and this would be a painfully slow process. He had to be sure of the depth, for if the water was deeper than the chart showed then the soldiers would leap off their landing craft into water above their heads. Heavily laden with equipment they would probably drown before a shot was fired.

The problems loomed large as his plan was expanded. How was he to get there? He decided a submarine was the obvious mode of transport, but that could not take him right up to the beach. He would have to paddle ashore in a dinghy. Then a fellow officer with experience of submarines pointed out that a bulky dinghy would not fit through the narrow torpedo hatch. But a canoe would! That would be it then, but the invasion was imminent and Willmott had never paddled a canoe in his life. He would have to enlist some help in mastering the technique of canoeing in a very short time.

Then there was the problem of keeping his equipment dry. An open canoe would take in water and the compass, torch and other paraphernalia vital to his reconnaissance would get wet and probably fail to function at the crucial time. He found a novel way of achieving this by enveloping each of the articles in navy issue contraceptives. So they had some use after all, he mused. Fortunately their manufacturer's boast that they would not burst was borne out when Willmott tested them in a basin of water. One problem solved—but a multitude more to overcome.

One of the prime difficulties was finding waterproof writing materials. He appreciated that he could not possibly commit all the information he gathered to memory and would have to make notes and sketches while in the water. Then there was the difficulty of taking soundings to determine the depth of the water on the approaches to the beach. He would simply have to walk inshore and determine the water's depth in relation to his own height. This would be an extremely lengthy and difficult process, especially right under the very noses of the enemy.

Among the thoughts that crammed his mind was his actual landing on the beach. A canoe could certainly take him so far but it would be cumbersome and would make him more easily seen on the beach. There was no doubt about it: he would have to get into the water and swim in. He could never hope to swim in from the submarine, carry out the reconnaissance then swim back out to rendezvous with it again. He would, he realised, have to take along a partner who would remain off-shore in the canoe while he swam ashore and got on with the job. The problem was, who would be 'lunatic' enough to embark on such a dangerous mission where the chances of survival were, to say the very least, minimal. He was to find such a man, to whom danger was almost a way of life. But Willmott's scheme was to be dealt a severe blow before that meeting took place.

To him, the sense of a pre-invasion reconnaissance was obvious, but the naval force commander did not share his enthusiasm when Willmott put forward the scheme to him. He just wouldn't wear it and gave the young Lieutenant Commander an emphatic 'no', pointing out that if he were discovered and captured on the beach, it might compromise the whole invasion plan. Willmott countered by saying that Naval Intelligence could give him a cover story; one that he could use if he happened to fall into the hands of the enemy. But his protests fell upon deaf ears. The answer was still no—the whole plan was too risky.

Undeterred by his superior's refusal, he carried on with his preparations, even going to the extent of rising at dawn every morning to engage in marathon bouts of swimming in the pool. In doing so he was toning up his muscles, keeping in trim and testing himself to the limit of his endurance. During these morning dips he practised the technique of 'silent' swimming using the end of the baths as an enemy shore, imagining an enemy sentry on duty there and perfecting the art of stealth in water.

It was the beginning of March and Willmott was convinced

beyond doubt that at any moment he would get an urgent summons from his chief to say that the 'show' was on. He had seen 'hair-brained' schemes put forward and turned down before, only to get top priority when the top brass realised how crucial they were to the overall plan. This instance proved no exception. Just as he had predicted, the summons came. It was fortunate that Willmott was a man of foresight and had continued his preparations, for the Force Commander ordered the reconnaissance mission to be carried out only two weeks from the day it was given the 'green light'.

Luckily by then Willmott had assembled most of the gear he would need for the mission: compasses, waterproof watches, seaproof torches and other bits and pieces he scrounged from reluctant colleagues. But with time fast running out, he had yet to persuade a companion with a good working knowledge of canoes to go with him and equally important, he had yet to find a commando-type canoe. It was the commander of the 1st Submarine Flotilla who suggested a way of finding both in one go. He advised Willmott to trace a commando officer by the name of Courtney.

Roger Courtney took little finding. He had been a legend even before his involvement with the commandos. Big game hunter, explorer and canoeist without peer, he was all of these things and more, a towering giant of a man abounding with muscle and of great physical strength, who lived on a diet of danger and revelled in it. This massive man had an equally enormous sense of humour. Big in stature and big in heart, it was he who had voyaged the length of the River Nile by canoe to reach the Victoria Falls. He had discovered a novel means of going on safari, by hunting big game from the cockpit of his canoe!

A great shambling ox of a man, Courtney's gait belied the swiftness of reflex inherent in the hunter. He was the antithesis of Willmott, whom he dwarfed. Willmott, the careful planner, the studious intellectual, left nothing to chance, while Courtney revelled in the element of risk attached to any commando operation. When the Lieutenant Commander tracked Courtney down, he found him living under canvas at a commando encampment on the fringe of the Great Bitter Lake, a car's drive from Cairo. Courtney clasped the sailor's hand in a vice-like grip of greeting. No time was wasted on preliminaries. Willmott outlined his plan and the gleam in the commando's eyes told him he had found his man. Courtney willingly offered him a canoe and all the help he could give, but there was a condition—He went with the canoe. Willmott was delighted. He had hesitated about asking Courtney to volunteer. There was a more than fifty-fifty chance that the mission would be a one-way trip but now he had a canoe and a volunteer itching to get on with the job.

The fact that Willmott had had no experience of canoes did not seem to perturb the redoutable Courtney in the slightest. A trial run was arranged for that afternoon and Willmott found himself sitting in the rear cockpit of a canvas cover twin commando canoe. The massive human frame in front of him seemed to overshadow the slender craft. Courtney's muscular arms manipulated the twin paddles with practised expertise, thrusting the canoe over the water with ease. Throughout the afternoon, Willmott was subjected to a crash course in the handling of a canoe. Courtney demonstrated the technique of silent paddling and on the mirror-like surface of the lake there was hardly a ripple or a sound as the canoe swiftly sped across it.

At the end of the afternoon, Willmott giddily disembarked from the craft, very impressed by its performance. But even so, there were still niggling little worries in the back of his mind. There was, it appeared, no problem in handling a canoe on the glassy surface of a quiet lake, but how would it stand up to the turbulent coastal waters off Rhodes? Characteristically Courtney brushed aside his partner's concern, but Willmott the worrier was not so easily satisfied. In the years to come, his concern was to be vindicated.

Throughout the time left to them before the departure of their submarine, the two men threw themselves into an intense programme of round-the-clock training and practice sessions, upon Willmott's insistence, and much against Roger Courtney's judgement.

Among the greatest hazards they were likely to face off Rhodes was the cold. Willmott estimated that he would have to spend at least four hours in the water reaching the beach and taking soundings. Without proper protection against cold, he could perish. After lengthy debate, Willmott and Courtney decided upon a comic but effective garb which they duly put to the test. They wore thick woollen sweaters and long underpants thickly smeared with grease which helped insulate them against the cold. The two men, resplendent in their apparel and resembling some Wellsian creatures from outer space, crept, crawled and sneaked around selected beaches in Egypt. While one acted as sentry, the other would attempt to penetrate the other's territory. After several nights, this technique had been perfected to such an extent that Willmott could get within touching distance of Courtney without the commando hearing or seeing him. The results of these night exercises were heartening but still Willmott insisted upon the training continuing at an exhausting pace, which did not go down at all well with Courtney who complained bitterly that they were overdoing it.

Throughout the hours of darkness their training continued. They practised signalling with torches. There were two important link-ups to make: Willmott with the canoe and the canoe with the submarine. To achieve this they used their sea-proof torches. Again and again Willmott left the canoe off-shore with Courtney holding it in position, and swam to the shore to carry out mock soundings. Using his torch and a prearranged signal he would flash and Courtney would home in on him. A more sophisticated homing device was to be used to rendezvous with the submarine, but that was to come later. Their will-o'-the-wisp activities continued until the eleventh hour. While all the preliminaries were being attended to, Willmott found time to liaise with Naval Intelligence who concocted a cover story. If either he or Courtney were unfortunate enough to fall into the hands of the enemy, they were to claim that they had been aboard a motor torpedo boat which had struck a mine and sunk. Both men were in no doubt as to the necessity for absolute secrecy. If their cover story were to be 'blown', it could well jeopardise the entire operation.

On the appointed date of departure, they arrived at Alexandria harbour and boarded the submarine *Triumph* while their canoe was slid inboard through the forward torpedo hatch. Soon the submarine was under way, sliding northward on the surface, en route for Rhodes. Courtney had hoped for some brief respite before the actual mission, but Willmott had quite different ideas. As the submarine sailed on, they went over their drill time and time again. Courtney protested—but Willmott insisted. Despite the dangers that would face them during the actual operation, Courtney longed to get on with it. Anything was preferable to Willmott's interminable rehearsals.

At last the submarine was nosing into the range of Italian aircraft and her commander took her down into the depth to slip undetected towards Rhodes. When they were within a few miles of the island, the submarine broke the surface to recharge her batteries. It was midnight and the process of revitalising her power-plant lasted until dawn. Towards sunrise Willmott clambered up into the control tower to take a look at the island on which he was to land the next night. The expanse of land was bathed in early morning light and it held a singular beauty which belied the menace on and beyond its shores.

As the sun began to appear, the boat's commander ordered her to dive and she slipped beneath the surface to become engulfed in the blue waters. Probing the water at periscope depth *Triumph* crept closer to the island shore to give Willmott a daylight view of his target for that night. The slender finger of the boat's periscope poked up through the surface. Below, in the control room, Willmott peered into the lens. His hands gripped the two protruding handles and he slowly panned the instrument. Like the eye of a cyclops the periscope traced the coastline of the island. The complex system of powerful lenses threw the coastline into revealing magnification. The island was awakening. Soldiers and Greeks went about their business. Army trucks cast up dust as they sped down a dusty road which wound through hills in the background to a town at the sea front. A gleaming white hotel dominated the beach; once the retreat of the wealthy, it was now the Axis headquarters.

Willmott searched the hills surrounding the small township which was partially obscured by a headland. His gaze passed along their undulating contours, hardly noticing the three growing dots in the sky 'inches' above the hill crests. The 'scope's eye almost casually passed them by, then Willmott whipped it back to focus upon the dots once more.

'Aircraft!' he snapped. 'Down periscope.'

The submarine commander's reaction was instant 'Dive! Dive! Dive!' *Triumph*'s bows dipped and she sloped down, seeking safety in the depths. A submarine was clearly visible from the air up to depths of 60 feet in the clear waters of the Aegean. The three aircraft, Italian Caprionis, carried bombs and as the submarine planed down everyone on board waited in breathless expectation for the first explosion. But the aircraft passed over the submarine's position and winged on out to sea. *Triumph* had not been seen but she was to be dogged by intense air activity for the rest of the day as she continued her periscope reconnaissance of the beaches earmarked for the landings. Enemy aircraft swept overhead and out across the Aegean to menace Allied convoys on their way to North Africa. It was precisely this menace that the invasion of Rhodes was intended to eliminate.

Between the alarms that punctuated the day, the submarine slid along the coast and Willmott got a close-up view of the town that lay partially hidden by the promontory. The town overlooked a small harbour which was protected by the projecting, curved arm of a mole with a defence boom at its tip. Within the harbour lay fast motor torpedo boats with their crews fussing about the decks, perhaps preparing for a patrol. Willmott took particular note of these nippy craft. They could cause him problems during his reconnaissance and equally wreak havoc among an invading force of landing craft. He was determined to have a closer look at them that night.

By mid-afternoon he had seen enough for the moment. The information he had gleaned so far had to be committed to paper, along with the sketches and notes he would make from his personal reconnaissance, to be pored over back in Cairo. *Triumph*'s captain took her deep to lie doggo until nightfall when the first of Willmott's sojourns ashore would take place.

Shortly after dark, *Triumph* rose to the surface once again, this time to recharge her batteries which were running low again. The throb of her diesels seemed to Willmott like a fanfare to wake the enemy, and the lengthy process of recharging interminable. He began to worry. Valuable hours of darkness were being eaten up while fresh power flowed into the batteries. Time that he could have been spending on the beach was slipping away. Willmott's biggest worry was the rendezvous with the submarine when his beach survey was complete. It would be perilously close to dawn and if he and Courtney missed the sub on the 'first pass', their canoe would easily be seen from the air.

At last the time for their departure drew near and they donned their gear and saturated themselves in a thick coating of grease. Their bodies gleamed like scaly fish and their comic appearance forced a toothy grin on their blackened faces. However, the humour of the moment was short-lived. Both realised that this first expedition might well be their last.

With the final touches made to their 'make-up' and their gear checked, they got the call to go on deck and emerged into the cold night air. Already the deck crew was manhandling their canoe out of the forward torpedo hatch. Hurried farewells were exchanged between them and *Triumph*'s captain, then they descended on to the deck as the submarine slid forward under battery power. The hum of the electric motors and the lapping of the sea against the casing were the only sounds that broke the silence of the night. The two men edged their way along the deck, past the gun platform with its crew standing ready, scanning the sea for the slightest hint of intruders. Willmott and Courtney soon reached the bows.

In the control tower *Triumph*'s captain issued orders in muted tones. The submarine slowed to a crawl. She was a mere four miles off the coast of Rhodes which sat squat and forbidding off the beam. The lights of the town twinkled in the distance. Willmott cast a glance towards his objective, allowing himself a moment's distraction to ponder upon what lay in store for him there. By then he and Courtney had reached the canoe, which was held fast by two sturdy seamen. *Triumph* was trimming down so that the canoe could be floated off. The deck became awash. The seamen lay on the flat hydroplane fin and held on to the canoe. On deck, commando and sailor poised to drop into their craft. The water swept over the two seamen as they battled to keep a grip on the canoe, then Willmott dropped into his cockpit followed a moment later by Courtney. The slim boat jinked crazily under the impact of the Commander's bulk, but it did not topple. Their paddles were handed down to them and they struck out towards the island. Before long the submarine was gone beneath a flurry of bubbling water.

Neither canoeist spoke as they dug their paddles into the sea and the canoe cut through the water towards the island. They made good headway until they reached some turbulent water which forced the canoe into a series of frightening gyrations. Both fought to keep the craft head on to the waves. The effort made both men sweat under their cocoon of grease and they panted breathlessly under the strain. At last they broke free of the turmoil into calmer waters, then the going became easier.

In the forward cockpit Willmott fixed his eyes upon the black land mass ahead. The coast which had been starkly clear in the sunlit day was now dark, the buildings silhouetted against a frowning sky. Few lights blinked in the houses. As they progressed, even these went out.

Willmott pinpointed the roadway that led down to the town when a car followed its course, headlights blazing. Then they paused. Willmott rescued his torch from its 'sheath' and shone it on to the rough outline sketch of the coast he had made the day before. By comparing this with the hazy outline before him, he was able to confirm that he was on course to land where he had planned.

It was then that the low groan of an aircraft's engines stirred the two men. The sound came from out at sea and grew in a deafening crescendo as a bomber roared over their heads to land on Rhodes. More aircraft followed, but the two intruders had no cause for concern as they headed towards the shore, cloaked in darkness. Thrusting on, they rounded the promontory until the town lay before them. The few lights that had shone earlier had been doused and the cluster of buildings lay black and still. The only craft they could see in the harbour were fishing vessels riding lazily at anchor. The MTBs which had been there earlier were gone, perhaps on patrol. It occurred to Willmott that an embarrassing and dangerous moment might come if these boats chose to return while they were lingering near the harbour mouth. But the lack of activity in the harbour indicated the scant probability of this happening. Emboldened by the lack of movement in the town, Willmott and Courtney ventured towards the harbour mouth. The mole towered ghostily white above them as they crept along the boom, straining their eyes to probe the secrets of the harbour. Only the water stirred. They could detect no signs of life on the land, no sentry who might catch a glimpse of them and awaken the sleepy town with an alarm. Even so, they dared not risk even a whisper and Willmott signalled that they were to move to the headland. Dipping their paddles into the water, they struck out for the promontory.

When he had viewed this jutting arm of land through the periscope earlier that day, Willmott had earmarked it as a possible landing point for part of the amphibious force. But he had to be sure that the foreshore would take the weight of tanks and that there were no obstructions that would impede the swift passage of

tanks on to the land. The beach itself was not the only consideration. There was little point in landing tanks or any other armoured
vehicles on a beach if there were no suitable exits from it. There
was only one way Willmott could find this out, and that was by
going ashore and looking for himself. A bare hundred yards
separated them from the shore when Willmott motioned to
Courtney to stop. Both men were bathed in sweat from the exertion of paddling. That and the tension had taken a toll of their
strength but now Willmott had to press on. With Courtney main-
taining the canoe's balance, his companion slid into the water.
The shock of the icy cold water took the breath from him. He
groped wildly for the canoe and clung on, fighting for breath. The
grease had failed to insulate him and its added weight was a terrible burden. Gradually some feeling crept back into his body.

'See you later,' he whispered, and launched himself off towards
the shore in a breast stroke. He knew now that his daily exercises
in the Cairo swimming pool were not wasted. At an easy, steady
pace he drew near the island, his head dipping and rising as he
progressed. The water lapped over his head allowing him only a
blurred view of the land in front, but he soon caught the un-
mistakable sound of waves crashing on to the beach. Almost
there. He stopped and tried to stand up, feeling for the bottom
with his feet. They did not touch. He moved further in and tried
again. This time he found he could stand up on the rugged sea bed.
From there he waded forward, forging a way through the surf until finally he reached the beach.

The scene that presented itself on this part of the beach was dis-
appointing. There were big, jagged rocks which would stop tanks
in their tracks and cause problems for other vehicles. The ground
rose steeply behind the beach. The spot was definitely out for
tanks but he thought it might make a good landing point for commandos. They could cope with the slope without much difficulty.

Willmott took a look along the distant sweep of the beach. He
would have to find a more suitable landing place for the tanks.
The beach was narrow and made up of shingle. Behind it was a
low wall which skirted the coast road he had seen earlier through
the periscope. He decided to swim back out to sea again and view
the beach farther along from the angle at which the landing craft
would make their approach. He struck out once more, swimming
in a wide arc until he trod water to see the beach. Then he headed

towards it. A few yards from the shore, he felt for the shingle with his feet and continued to do so until he crawled into the waves that lapped the shore. The strength sapped out of him, he lay wallowing in the frothy surf, allowing it to tumble over him and refresh him.

Willmott rolled over on his back, his chest heaving after the exertion of the swim. Then his heart leapt and he froze. The sound of voices reached his ears, clearly audible over the rustle of the water on the shingle. Gingerly he turned over on his stomach and chanced a look up towards the road. Close by the wall were two figures, unmistakably German soldiers with their 'coal-scuttle' helmets and rifles slung over their shoulders. The low, intermittent guttural tones confirmed their nationality. Willmott lay transfixed. He and Courtney had practised for events such as this but no amount of practice could have prepared him for the cold terror of the real thing. The force of the waves assaulting the beach drove him inches forward each time they hit, nudging him nearer to the sentries. Their backs were to him and he prayed that they would move off without looking his way. This was the critical moment, the moment when a whole invasion could be ruined. Wild thoughts raced through his mind; if he were caught, would his cover story convince his interrogators? If not, would he succumb under torture; would he blurt out the whole story? Thousands of men's lives depended on him—but wasn't that why he had come? No, he tried to convince himself, he wouldn't get caught. He and Courtney had gone through this many times before. They had proved that it could be done. A few seconds later that theory was put to the ultimate test. Willmott's eyes glared as one of the sentries turned and looked towards him. An icy chill gripped him as he lay in the surf, willing the sentry to mistake him for a rock. The German seemed to gaze in his direction for an age, then turned and strolled out of sight with his companion.

Willmott had to get into the shadow of the wall and he squirmed farther up the beach, making his moves each time the waves rolled up the shingle. The movement of his body was covered by the sound of the shingle as it was cast forward then drawn back by the breaking waves. At last his hands touched barbed wire. A long entanglement stretched the length of the wall. With hands trembling from the cold, he lifted the wire and eased himself under it until finally he was through.

Willmott crouched by the wall, pausing a while before making his next move, then slowly raising himself to peer over the rim of the wall. The two sentries were no more than ten yards from where he crouched. They stood talking in low tones. But then he detected the sound of an approaching vehicle. Willmott ducked just in time to avoid being caught in the beam of its headlights as they swept the wall. The car roared past without stopping and the noise died. This was no place to linger. Wilimott had seen enough.

Lack of strenuous activity had allowed the cold to penetrate his sodden clothing. He was chilled through and trembled uncontrollably but he had to retrace his steps back to the sea. Again he found his way under the barbed wire then began to elbow across the shingle towards the surf. He collapsed in a jelly-like quaking heap, unable to move any farther. No amount of will or determination could steady his quivering body and he had no alternative but to allow it to overtake him. He relaxed as his body shook then he forced himself up onto his elbows and once more fought forward. The water engulfed him bringing another intense shock of cold. He set himself to swimming again and the motion of his limbs brought some degree of warmth back to him. It was as he struggled out into the darkened sea that he caught sight of what appeared to be a gun emplacement. He made towards it, only to find that it was a diving platform. Even in his incredibly weakened state, the humour of his mistake was not lost upon him.

His job was by no means done. To ensure that the beach was suitable for a landing, he had to systematically sound its length and by a miracle of will, he set about it, making his way in to the shore, testing it for depth then retreating, moving farther along repeating the process.

The effort of swimming brought back a drenching sweat which mingled with the freezing cold water that saturated him but he continued his exhausting task, all the time keeping an eye open for sentries on the road. At last he reached a shoal which he knew could mean disaster for the landing craft. He felt his way along it to determine its length before finally arriving at deep water once more. Now he knew the safe landing areas for the craft on that beach. He had one more objective—to scout the hotel which dominated that stretch of the coast.

In spite of Willmott's incredible trials in the sea and on the beach, it was perhaps Courtney who had the more testing job of the two. At least Willmott was active; he could see where dangers lay and take evasive action. But Courtney had to play the waiting game, remaining in position for three long hours, not knowing what had become of his friend, unable to help if Willmott got into trouble, not knowing if he would return.

Courtney was by no means unaccustomed to danger—but he was a man of action, one who had always been in the van of the attack. There was little time to feel fear in the heat of the battle. Indeed action itself drove him on. But this was something quite different, alien to his character and he felt edgy and ill at ease. As the minutes of waiting became hours he began to suffer from hallucinations; every lap of water upon the canoe's sides jolted him; the slightest stir sent a cold shiver down his spine. Damn, he thought, if only he could *do* something. The quiet of the placid sea and dark hump of land nearby took on an eerie, almost ghostly hue. A mental spectre haunted his brain and his imagination ran riot. At any moment he expected the island to erupt in a blaze of gun fire but even that would have been some relief. He tried moving his position, just to be active and in a bid to exorcise that spirit of cold fear that was overwhelming him. But it did not work. Finally he was overcome by nausea and vomited into the sea. The sickness purged him of a little of his uneasiness and he continued to wait with something vaguely approaching renewed optimism. But his concern for Willmott would not leave him.

Meanwhile Willmott was nearing the beach again. Ahead of him the hotel loomed large, its lawn spreading like an apron in front of it. This imposing white building housed the enemy's senior officers on the island and it was bound to be heavily guarded. More caution than ever would be needed now. Breathless after his swim, Willmott slipped on to the beach, moving cautiously up it. His eyes scanned the low wall. No sentries visible, but that did not mean they were not there, lurking in the shadows. He paused for a moment and listened. Silence.

The hotel was in darkness but there *were* sentries about—he could hear them now. The occasional cough, sigh or shuffle of feet betrayed their presence. From behind the shrubbery where he hid, Willmott could hear one humming a low tune, another pacing along the front of the hotel. Another took time out to 'water' the lawn. Willmott noted their positions, then darted into the cover of another bush, moving with the silence of a stalking predator, despite his sodden clothing. His eyes strained to penetrate the darkness and discover hidden defences, the sort of gun emplacements that could wipe out a sizable chunk of a raiding force. With a fleetness of foot which was incredible in view of his physical state he completed his reconnaissance and stole back to the beach. But now he had to find Courtney.

Willmott had been separated from his companion for some three hours. Dawn was not far off and if they failed to link up before then, there was little doubt that they would be spotted and killed or captured. But he consoled himself with the thought that if anything had happened to Courtney, he would certainly have heard something.

Every stroke of Willmott's arms demanded Herculean effort. He aimed to swim about two hundred yards off shore, then use his torch to signal to Courtney but his arms and legs were numbed almost to immobility with cold and exhaustion, and the awful prospect of drowning filled his mind. He found himself floundering. If he missed Courtney he knew he would not have the strength to make it back to the shore.

After only a short distance, he could go on no longer. He trod water but repeatedly sank and took in mouthfuls of bitter salt water. Summoning his fast waning strength, he managed to find his torch. He lifted it above his head and had to battle with the button to switch it on. Mercifully it shone and he waved it out to sea, begging Courtney to catch a glimpse of it. The thought did occur to him that an enemy boat might spot the flashes and reach him first, but he was so weak that this prospect hardly seemed to matter any longer.

For ten minutes Willmott continued waving his beacon in an arc out to sea. He had almost given up hope when at last he heard the sound of Courtney's paddles pushing the canoe towards him. The commando drew alongside and with eager hands helped to heave Willmott up on to the boat. He lay spreadeagled across the canoe for a while, catching his breath, until he was able to scramble into his cockpit. Courtney passed him a flask of whisky and he gulped down a mouthful. The spirit burned like hell as it percolated through his system, then he took a swig from a flask of coffee. Slowly some vestige of life came back to him and the two men turned their thoughts to the rendezvous with *Triumph*.

Each of them raised a paddle and dipped it into the sea. The canoe slid forward, cutting a path through the water. With the prospect of rest in the submarine, they built up a steady pace—but their troubles were by no means over. The undulating sea took on a flat calm and soon they became shrouded in thick fog, dense and wet. Now the chance of a rendezvous with the submarine became precarious indeed. How could they possibly be spotted in this murk? Their state of mind, already strained after their night's ordeal, took a plunge. They could paddle around in the fog for hours without making headway or contact with *Triumph*. The fog had descended upon the coast in a series of banks and the canoeists emerged from one layer, only to become engulfed in another. Using his compass, Willmott was able to keep the canoe heading out to sea until they were clear of the fog that hugged the island.

The canoe detached itself from the screen of fog and the two adventurers found themselves on a calm sea beneath a canopy of stars. Their relief was enormous and they both had a strong pull at the flask of whisky to celebrate. But there was no time to linger and they pressed on. It was now that a sophisticated infra-red homing device was to come to their aid. It seemed curiously out of place among their other improvised equipment but it was nonetheless a life-saver. It comprised a transmitter and receiver, the transmitter to send out a signal to *Triumph* and the receiver to take the submarine's signal which was displayed as a green blob on a small screen.

Courtney 'swept' the sea with the transmitter while Willmott's eyes were glued to the receiver screen. For five long minutes nothing appeared on the screen. Then suddenly a green blob lit up on it—it was *Triumph*. They'd found her. Moments later the submarine broke the surface like a huge whale and they were taken aboard to collapse into warm bunks.

The night's events had drained them of energy and they slept soundly, regaining their stamina. They were to need it, for the following night another beach had to be reconnoitred, and yet another the night after.

Still suffering from the ordeal of the previous night, Willmott went ashore again to survey a second beach. If anything his experiences this time were even worse, for he started out tired and he suffered the hallucinations that had plagued Courtney the night before. But he had learned a few tricks and the reconnaissance was completed and the information gathered. But by then Willmott had had enough. He was physically and mentally drawn to the point of near collapse and it was agreed that Courtney would undertake the beach reconnaissance on the third night, while Willmott waited off-shore for him. Although not as physically spent as his naval companion, Courtney almost did not make it back to the canoe. He was caught by the fierce grip of cramp and could not swim. Luckily for him, Willmott risked all to come in shore and found him then took him off, otherwise Courtney might have had to be left on the island.

The following morning Willmott wanted a last look at one of the beaches through the submarine's periscope, despite an urgent order from Cairo to return at once. Through the 'scope, he clearly detected two gun emplacements at either end of the beach which would have murdered an invading force. All the while the submarine was nosing further in towards the shore. Then suddenly it ground to a halt. The boat shuddered and seemed to surge upwards. To the captain's horror, he realised that they had run aground and that the upper structure of the submarine must be exposed above the water. Frantically the orders were given to reverse engines and the boat trembled as it struggled to get free. Every moment they expected the shore batteries to open up but mercifully they remained silent. *Triumph* wriggled free and dived deep then set course for Alexandria. They had tempted fate just far enough for one mission.

Back in Alexandria, Willmott set himself to making sense out of all the intelligence he had gleaned during the reconnaissance. He worked like a demon. There was more than just the invasion at stake; he was determined to prove the necessity and feasability of pre-invasion surveys once and for all. These should become an accepted procedure. The potential menaces Willmott had uncovered on and around the shores of Rhodes had proved to him without a shadow of doubt that his conviction was right. He now had the evidence to support this—the results of the reconnaissance plus the safe arrival back of Courtney and himself. In addition, and every bit as important, the whole operation had been carried out without the enemy suspecting a thing. Willmott was in very high spirits as he put the finishing touches to a mound of accumulated intelligence. But his justifiable elation was about to be dashed. The crushing news came in just two words—'INVASION CANCELLED'.

To anyone other than Willmott the cancellation of the invasion might have been just too much to bear. When he first heard the news, he was thunderstruck, unable to believe that the meticulous planning, the exhausting effort expended and the danger that had been endured, had all been for nothing. But that initial shock and disappointment was soon tempered with the academic's philosophical reasoning. The course of the war in the desert had taken a turn for the worse with the arrival of the German General Rommel and his crack Afrika Korps. The Allies were on the run, not only there but in Yugoslavia too. An invasion of Rhodes was now out of the question.

Courtney and Willmott parted company, the sailor to be given a roving commission and made available to almost anyone who might need him, Courtney to form the Special Boat Section of the commandos and get himself involved in some epic clandestine raids and reconnaissance missions on his favourite mount, the canoe. The formation of Courtney's new unit emphasized the Army's ready acceptance of pre-raid reconnaissance. However the Navy was not to share that enthusiasm—at least not for some time. For his courage on the Rhodes expedition, Willmott was admitted to the Distinguished Service Order and all his pre-invasion survey ideas 'shelved'. This attitude on the part of the Navy is perhaps understandable but hardly excusable. The Allies were at that time on the defensive. Invasions would have to wait—but they were to regret bitterly their lack of heed to Willmott's advice.

His roving commission was not however without its memorable moments. A commando raid was planned upon a recently-built German radar station on the island of Kupho which lay off the coast of Crete. Willmott was appointed to go ashore and lead in the boats carrying the commandos who would 'relieve' the station of its code books and blow it up. Remembering his experiences on Rhodes and in particular the unreliability of the available charts, Willmott realised that he would first have to go ashore himself then scout around for a suitable beach before signalling the landing craft in. To assist him in his task, the commandos provided him with a refugee from the island of Kupho, one Antonopoulo by name.

This Cretan had an overwhelming zest for life—but was possessed with two qualities guaranteed to ruin any secret mission; he was an inveterate boaster—and he was given to doing it loudly, to boot. To him the mission was 'a walkover'. He had been born and bred on Kupho and knew every inlet, creek, beach and grain of sand upon it. Willmott was sceptical of the man's ability to tell the truth but decided that, since he was a native of the island, he might be of some help and agreed to take him along. However, so much depended upon the element of surprise being achieved in the raid and absolute secrecy observed before the raid that Willmott decided the Cretan would have to be 'gagged', at least until they were underway. So, no sooner had Antonopoulo been 'signed on' than he was arrested and unceremoniously cast into jail on a trumped up charge of drunkenness. He was furious and subjected his captors to a blazing tirade of invective. Only a few hours before their departure, Willmott 'bailed him out' and they boarded one of the two destroyers that were to take them and the raiding parties to Kupho.

The bows of the destroyers sliced through the sea on their way for the small island but throughout the voyage Willmott became aware of a marked change in the Cretan's demeanour. He became increasingly silent and was given to spending long periods deep in thought with furrowed brow. Perhaps it was only to be expected, Willmott thought. After all the man was returning to the homeland from which he had been exiled and it must be an emotional experience for him. How wrong that supposition was to be!

The two destroyers arrived in the Aegean and lay well off the coast of Kupho while a dinghy was lowered with Willmott, Antonopoulo and a seaman aboard. While the seaman rowed the dinghy towards the black island which was only just visible in the distance, Willmott realised that Antonopoulo's metamorphosis was complete. Not only had he gone quiet, but Willmott could not prise a word out of him. The Cretan's face was a mere silhouette but his uneasy fidgeting in the stern of the dinghy indicated to Willmott that he was terrified.

Gradually they drew closer to the island. Now was the time to make use of his reluctant passenger. Willmott turned to him. The man was shaking nervously but Willmott asked him in which direction they should steer. Silence. Willmott impatiently repeated the question. In a voice quaking with fear, Antonopoulo admitted that he did not know. Not only did he not know—he had never been to this part of the island before!

Willmott found it difficult to restrain himself from yelling at the man. He simply stared at him in stark disbelief while Antonopoulo slid to the bottom of the boat, pleading with Willmott to take him home. The seaman at the oars paused, not quite knowing whether the mission was on or off. By now the Cretan was crying. Willmott threatened him with a fate worse than death if he did not 'shut up' and this at least muted his sobbing but he remained a quaking wreck in the well of the boat.

Willmott ordered the oarsman to continue and they nudged closer to the island. He could now hear the waves lapping the shore and as they drew nearer, Willmott could just make out a small beach. A little way off-shore he told the oarsman to stop rowing and gave him explicit instructions as to what to do if the Cretan uttered another sob. With that Willmott slipped over the side of the dinghy and swam to the shore. He crawled onto a cove embraced by cliffs. The beach seemed to be okay for a landing but first he had to make sure that there was at least one exit from it for the commandos. In fact he found two routes, and no sentries or gun emplacements after his quick reconnoitre, so he headed back out to the boat once more.

Willmott waded out to the boat then they pulled away out to sea. When he was a suitable distance off shore, he flashed a signal to the waiting destroyers and the cutters with their Marine Commandos on board soared forward. From the dinghy Willmott could hear them coming, then they came into sight, squat boats coursing through the waves. Inside them, groups of commandos huddled, trigger fingers poised on their weapons, alert and ready for action.

The fight came sooner than anticipated. With the suddenness of a thunderflash, the horse-shoe curve of cliffs erupted in a withering hail of fire. From positions on the cliff-top, German gunners opened up at the oncoming cluster of cutters. Machineguns chattered in a rasping fusillade of fire. Bullets zipped into the sea, peppering its darkness with tiny spurts of phosphorescence. They ripped into the boats, wounding and killing and splintering the wooden hulls. But still the commandos forged on.

The boats lurched onto the beach and black figures leapt from them, hurling themselves like greyhounds up the thin strip of sand, their weapons spitting fire at the German positions on the cliff top. From his seat in the stalls, Willmott watched the drama unfold. Against the jet backcloth of the looming cliffs, a cobweb pattern of multi-coloured tracer bullets laced the sky as the exchange of fire grew in intensity. The commandos were gaining a toe-hold on the shore. Then the roar of the fight moved inland, punctuated by the vicious crack of grenade explosions.

The fury of the fight seemed to die then pause expectantly as if waiting for a cataclysmic climax. It came with a stark flash that momentarily threw the island into jagged relief and bathed the cloud base high above in orange light. It struck Willmott like the shutter of a camera opening and closing for a fraction of a second and leaving an imprint upon the eye.

The radar station lay in ruins behind the commandos as they scurried towards the shore. A group of them bore the burden of the safe containing the code books that had been wrested from the radar station before it was blown up. Ringed by a shield of commandos who fired at the slightest stir, the safe breakers made for the beach with their precious prize.

Willmott saw them clamber aboard their boats while a rearguard kept the Germans' heads down. His job was done and Willmott made out towards the waiting destroyers with the cutters following in his wake. The safe was secure—the raid a success. Antonopoulo was jubilant and Willmott was satisfied. But a crushing blow was to be dealt them. As the cutter containing the safe was being hoisted up on to its destroyer, one of the ropes broke, the boat tilted and the safe fell into the sea—where it might well rest to this day.

Gaining the security of the destroyer's deck, Antonopoulo's verbosity returned with a vengeance and his 'heroic' part in the raid was related in varying versions to any luckless seaman with a willing ear. Willmott had not the heart to deny the Cretan his moment of glory. Doubtless Antonopoulo's courage that night will go down in Cretan legend—and more than match that of other mythological heroes.

The Kupho raid was but a solitary interlude in an otherwise humdrum year for Willmott. The Royal Navy had, for reasons best known to itself, pigeon-holed Willmott's experiences at Rhodes for future reference. More than twelve months were to elapse before his expertise was to be called upon again, this time for an invasion that paled the Rhodes adventure into insignificance—'Operation Torch', the Anglo-American invasion of French North Africa. It was to be the first full-scale Allied amphibious invasion of the war and one of massive dimensions. Willmott returned to England in May 1942 and was appointed to Combined Operations, an organisation comprising specialists from all three Services, which conceived some of the great and daring raids of the war under the leadership of Lord Louis Mountbatten. It was now faced with the awesome task of planning the British participation in 'Operation Torch'. Willmott was summoned to give vent to his feelings upon the subject of the actual landings and how, with his experience at Rhodes behind him, he thought this could best be achieved with the minimum loss of landing craft and life. Talking to an imposing array of 'gold braid', he stressed the necessity for beach reconnaissance, pointing out in as forceful terms as he dared that without it, the amphibious landing force might well be doomed. As he talked, his eyes searched the faces of every senior officer seated before him, who listened intently. They absorbed Willmott's dialogue and each occasionally nodded in agreement with what he said. They could hardly do much else. Willmott's diatribe made sense. Finally he sat down. There were a few whispered mutterings and joining of heads, then the Lieutenant Commander was dismissed—and so it seemed was his plan.

While the details of Operation Torch were attended to, Willmott waited for the go-ahead. Days passed into months. He had no idea when the invasion was to take place but he estimated that it had to come soon. Activity at Combined Headquarters was reaching fever pitch and he saw the whole jigsaw of the operation begin to knit into place—but still there was no hint of his being called to plan a reconnaissance. He feared that, as had happened before on the Rhodes excursion, he would be remembered at the eleventh hour, when only a hastily contrived reconnaissance could be carried out. True to form, an urgent summons came from the Staff Navigator to the invasion force. He wanted to know all Willmott had learned about the art of beach reconnaissance. Patiently, he explained. Being a navigator himself, the staff man quickly grasped the seriousness of the situation—and ordered Willmott to prepare a report on his recommendations and have it in writing ready for presentation to the Chief of Staff *the following morning!*

Willmott had been expecting something like this and had already formulated a plan of action in his mind but he had to spend that night burning the midnight oil to get the whole scheme down on paper. Bleary-eyed and tired after his night's work, he presented his report. Within the hour, he was wakened from a restless sleep by another urgent summons. Things were beginning to move fast. The report had been read and now the top brass wanted him to elaborate upon certain points in it. The exhausted Willmott duly did so and it was then that he learned he was to have less than two months in which to build up a reconnaissance force capable of not only carrying out a pre-raid survey of five assault beaches but also leading in the amphibious landing craft with their troops and armour. It was early November and the invasion was planned for mid-December. In that space of time he had to recruit, train and equip his unit, find five submarines, a sufficient number of suitable commando canoes, as well as all the paraphernalia vital to such an operation. In addition to all this, he had to have cover stories worked out for his teams lest they should fall into the hands of the enemy. (Willmott's personal theory on the subject of discovery was that if it happened, his men were to fight their way out of trouble—or die. The secrecy of their operation had to be preserved, even at the cost of their lives.)

He was given Top Priority and he wasted not a moment in launching himself into the formidable task of organisation but first he committed the plan in detail to paper, working out his requirements to ensure that every possible eventuality was considered and taken into account.

Willmott's first and most urgent consideration was the recruitment of men. They would be difficult to find. He would have to persuade navigators, who were worth their weight in gold, away from important jobs to join him and he realised even then that he was bound to incur the displeasure of certain senior officers who jealously guarded their priceless possessions. He planned to enlist three navigators and the help of his old friend Courtney. He, along with his group, would fly out to Gibraltar, make their way to the invasion beaches by submarine and then use canoes to land on the beaches and carry out detailed surveys.

When this had been done, Willmott's force of 'markers' comprising sailors and commandos from Courtney's Special Boat

Section, would be launched from submarines to light the way in for the landing craft. In essence, the plan was simple, but in reality, it was a formidable prospect.

When he had compiled his list of personnel, it was forwarded to the appropriate authority so that the recruitment could begin—and it found its way to Mountbatten himself. It appeared that he was demanding a sizeable chunk of the Combined Operations strength, and Mountbatten wanted to know the reason why. Willmott was summoned to appear before him and explain. He did so and Mountbatten, with the clarity of a brilliant leader, conceded—but it was to be almost another week before Willmott was given the all-clear to go ahead with his plan. In that time it was scrutinised by senior officers who had their own questions to ask before giving it their personal stamp of approval. With every day vital to him, Willmott found that week a particularly frustrating one. When permission was finally given, Willmott learned that the number of invasion beaches was to be increased, which meant recruiting even more officers and men, finding more canoes and indeed more of everything.

Willmott had no difficulty whatsoever in obtaining the canoes. He went to Courtney, who simply told him to 'help himself'. Then Willmott tentatively broached the question of getting commando officers and men. Again, Courtney was magnanimous and Willmott picked five commando officers and men. Courtney counted himself in on the operation but when he asked leave of his superiors to join Willmott he got a curt and definite 'no'.

Now things sped ahead at a firey pace. Willmott rounded up his officers and men and assembled them at the main submarine base HMS *Dolphin* at Fort Blockhouse in Portsmouth. Crammed into a room, he addressed his assembled force for the first time and outlined what the job entailed, leaving out nothing of the hazard involved. Then he gave them the opportunity of backing out if they felt they were not cut out for such an undertaking. None of them did.

The task of training the new unit was to be difficult enough, but the biggest obstacle Willmott faced in these hectic days was the seemingly impenetrable morass of red tape he had to unravel to get the equipment he so desperately needed for the operation. It quickly became apparent that the only way to get what he wanted was to sweep aside the red tape and demand the goods, if necessary at the top of his voice, brandishing his Top Priority authority. To his great frustration even this did not always sway reluctant storemen in his favour. As a result, a further week elapsed before he had enough equipment to begin the crucial training. Willmott was furious, because he and his beach reconnaissance team were due to leave for Gibraltar in just two weeks' time. This meant leaving the remainder of the team in England to continue their training under a new officer and without his (Willmott's) supervision. They would follow him out by sea a month later.

In the meantime, Willmott plunged them into a fierce and intensive period of training, which not only included mastering the techniques required of them as canoeists but also a rigorous toughening up programme. One of the most delicate of the skills they had to master was actually boarding the canoes from a submarine at sea. They had to jump down into the cockpits from the deck of the submarine and many of them came to grief when they first attempted it.

Willmott drove them on in their training programme like a tyrant. He knew and had experienced what they would face on the actual operation and spared nothing to shape them up for their ordeal. No matter what the weather, every officer and man was forced to swim naked over long distances. By night they practised the art of beach reconnaissance, often falling foul of patrolling sentries. On one occasion Willmott had to retrieve one of his men from jail after he had been arrested on the beach. The training was both physically and mentally exhausting. But that was the way Willmott had designed it. He drove his officers and men to the limit. There were many moments of intense fright for the canoeists when Willmott drove them out to sea in the most incredible weather conditions. There were those who saw their commander as a tyrannical slave-master, with an ingrained sadistic streak. Little were they to know then that their very lives were to depend upon this unremitting drive. There was to be no let-up either when Willmott flew off to Gibraltar with his beach scouts. The training back home was to be as intensive as ever.

Willmott and his team of beachcombers landed in Gibraltar amid a hive of activity. The Rock bustled with pre-invasion activity and Willmott had still to put the finishing touches to the training programme for his men before taking them across the

Mediterranean to North Africa. He planned to carry out the beach reconnaissances four days after their arrival when two submarines would be made available to him, one to take the canoes to the Oran beaches and the other to take them to the Algiers coast. But then an urgent signal came from the Admiralty *forbidding Willmott to land his men on the coast.* It appeared that they had got cold feet and saw the risk of their capture as possibly jeopardising the whole operation. Willmott took the other view—he reasoned that not landing to carry out a proper survey would be an even greater risk. Now he would have to make do with a periscope survey of the proposed beaches.

Reconnoitring the beaches at Algiers and Oran took somewhere around two weeks of peering at them through the periscopes of the two submarines and although the survey proved of some use in establishing hazards visible on the surface, Willmott was haunted by the prospect of what might lie beneath the waters lapping these shores.

When the two submarines arrived back at Gibraltar, Willmott found that the remainder of his unit had arrived from England, having suffered the rigours of a long and stormy voyage out. They were in a pitiful physical condition and Willmott set about rectifying this by an exhausting fitness training programme, which included daily runs up the Rock. After a few days of this toughening-up process, Willmott was pleased to see a marked improvement in their condition. But for him that was not enough. He ordered that on their runs they were now to wear full packs. The pace of these exercises was killing but they brought the unit to a high state of fitness. Still the gruelling exercises and canoeing continued and although there were many grumbles, none of them could seriously complain, for Willmott took part in all of them, as well as being involved in all the organisational problems. For him, 'rest' meant a couple of hours sleep grabbed on the rare occasions when time permitted. The pace was taking its toll of him and he looked and felt dreadful. But he never let up. The time of the invasion was drawing close.

Willmott planned that the markers should be taken to their beaches by the navigators and shown the exact positions they would have to hold to light the way in for the invaders. When the invasion proper began, the markers in their canoes would sit off the coast and flash torches out to sea. The main invasion force would home on submarines lying well out to sea and the invasion craft would be lowered. Each assault group of craft would take on board one of Willmott's navigators who would lead them towards the shore. The flashing of the marker's light would then direct them accurately on to the beach. That at least was the plan. Things were to go dreadfully awry.

Only two weeks after their arrival from England, they were due to sail. Every available ship and boat that could be spared from the Anglo-American navies was homing on the west Mediterranean for the invasion. There was almost four hundred of them, varying in size from battleships to landing craft and submarines. More than 600 aircraft were massed to fly cover for the invasion fleet. Thirteen submarines, other than those allocated to Willmott's unit, were standing sentinel off the Italian and French coast ready to intercept and sink any Axis warships that might put to sea in a bid to prevent the invasion.

While the mighty armada was making its way from ports in America and Britain to form up for the invasion, Willmott's submarines sailed. There were five of them, each carrying their allocated canoe crews and navigators, and they arrived off the North African coast two nights before the invasion was due to begin. The intention was to take the markers inshore to show them their beaches so that they knew exactly where they were to position themselves then return to the submarines and wait for the following night when they would go in alone.

When the submarines surfaced at Algiers to off-load their canoes, they found the weather had stirred into a storm, which not only made launching the canoes difficult but made the paddle towards the coast extremely hazardous. They had to suffer almost continuous drenching from the waves whipped up by a fierce wind and were forced to bale like madmen as the canoes took in water, to stop themselves sinking. The struggle against the elements was strength-sapping, and punctuated with some hair-raising experiences. Off Oran the canoe paddled by Magnall and Edwards slipped towards the shore. Here the water was quite calm, in fact too calm. They were not disturbed by the strong wind that was bedevilling the others off Algiers. But because of the placidity, they were more easily seen. They were tense and nervous of any movement in the sea around them. Ahead they could just discern the thin coastline. Suddenly the oily calm of the sea was broken by a flurry of bubbles. Both men's heads whipped round to focus on the disturbance. Their hearts leapt—then they saw the cause—a school of porpoises which had found the canoe a playful toy around which they soared and dipped in a series of graceful acrobatics. They were gone just as suddenly as they had appeared. Magnall and Edwards dipped their paddles once more and got under way.

They had gone only a few yards when another sound reached their ears through the stillness of the night; it was the low throb of an engine, off to starboard. Their eyes searched the shrouded sea, peering to pin-point the source of the sound. Slowly the silhouette of a small craft became visible. It was heading in their direction. Both men froze, not daring to move as the boat drew nearer to them. They willed her to change course but she kept thrusting on through the glassy surface of the sea. With a deft flick of a paddle, the canoeists turned stern on to the boat so as to present as slender a shape as possible. Then they groped for their guns, expecting at any moment to have a fight on their hands. By now the launch was no more than forty yards distant. Their discovery could be only moments away. But as the intruder came within thirty yards of them, the noise of the engines died and the boat stopped, with engine idling. No bullets whistled towards the canoe. No cry of alarm. Nothing. It was incredible that they had not been seen.

There seemed nothing they could do. Then, off to port, they heard the throb of another boat. The din of its engine grew and the canoeists realised that it was heading in their direction. Maybe, they thought, they had stumbled into a rendezvous point. Myriad thoughts raced through their minds. They had been unable to identify the first boat as either military or civilian. She might be a fishing boat, but equally she might be an enemy patrol boat, which was a greater likelihood.

Both men waited anxiously to catch sight of the second boat but they were to be denied that. Gradually the noise of the engine faded. She had changed course and was heading away from them. That at least was one less to worry about but they were still menaced by the vessel which lurked at their backs.

Neither man could dare a whisper to the other but both knew instinctively that they could not remain where they were. With the passing of each second their chances of being seen were increased. It was Edwards who made the first move. Cautiously he tapped

Magnall, indicating his intention to move off. Then with bated breath they gently dug their paddles into the water. The canoe glided forward. They chanced another thrust. The launch lay still, her engine gurgling. As the canoe split the calm of the water with her bows, putting more distance between it and the launch, Edwards and Magnall risked a few more powerful strokes. Forging forward they glanced around at the boat receding into the background until she was lost from view, then the canoe lunged forward like a whippet. They had escaped discovery by a hair's breadth. Not long afterwards, they were back on board their submarine, panting from exhaustion. There was no doubt that Willmott's unrelenting training had saved them from certain death or captivity.

Edwards and Magnall were not the only ones to get a severe fright that night. One of the other Oran canoes almost barged into a small fleet of fishing boats working off the coast near the invasion beach. Only by some clever manoeuvring did they escape discovery.

Other canoe crews were not to be so lucky. The fear that had haunted Willmott and persuaded his superiors not to allow personal beach surveys was justified. Two of his men were captured.

Two hundred miles east of Oran, near Algiers, were three beaches where landings were to take place. On that night, three submarines launched canoes to take a look at the beaches. Two of them got back safely through the violent storm that raged there. One did not. It was manned by Lieutenant Geoffrey Lyne, the navigator, and Thomas, his beach marker. A raging storm cast the sea into a torment, throwing up waves which towered above the two men, then caught them and hurtled them skyward. They fought to keep bow-on to the waves as they soared towards them. If the canoe were to twist beam on to the onrushing crest of water, they would be deluged and in all probability sunk. The strain on their arms was enormous and they battled and jockeyed on crest and in deep trough. The effort was made doubly difficult as the sea found its way into the canoe, threatening to swamp and sink it as the weight of water increased. Drenched, they struggled on, the wind whipping the waves into their faces, making vision a dim blur. The sea was winning the first skirmish in a bitter battle. The heaving sea caught the canoe in its grip and tightened its watery hand on the craft, driving it around in a wild corkscrew. As they spun in a lethal carousel, the light of the coast and the dark of the sea dazzled them until their dizzy heads reeled.

Mercifully there was a short lull while the sea summoned her strength for another onslaught. In that short space, they ripped the canvas cover off the canoe and baled like fury to empty her of the water that was swamping them. The water in the craft lapped over their legs but the baling gradually made an impression on it. Their equipment was drenched and only added to the weight of the craft. They realised they could never hope to face another fight with the elements with all their equipment on board so they tossed the Tommy gun overboard, along with their grenades and homing gear.

A glance at the coast told them that they had been swept far from their intended position and time was running out for their rendezvous with the submarine.

The wind drew a deep breath then exhaled. Again they were tossed into a turmoil of sea with precipitous cliffs of water looming over black troughs. For half an hour they waged war on the waves. Had it not been for their fitness they would already have succumbed, but they emerged into another lull in physically spent victory over the elements. They baled furiously having unhooked the canvas canopy once more but this time the sea and wind joined forces to catch them off guard. A mountainous wave crashed down on the open canoe, smothering it in water but, by some miracle, she did not sink. Lyne and Thomas emerged saturated and sitting in a canoe filled to the gunwales with water. They knew that they would never make it. Both men panned the water out of the canoe then Thomas signalled out to sea with his torch—but in their hearts they knew the effort was in vain. They were miles away from the rendezvous position with the submarine. But even with their brains and bodies numbed by cold and exhaustion, they continued to paddle, from time to time signalling out to sea in the hopeless belief that they might yet be spotted.

The storm continued throughout the night, buffetting them with its every movement. Finally dawn came, and with it, the storm subsided, leaving the two shattered shells of men humped and lifeless in their canoe. The craft followed the flow of the sea which gently took them farther away from the coast. As they drifted, Lyne tried to make some sense of their plight. He considered heading into the shore in the hope that they might land unseen upon a beach. But by now it was broad daylight and the canoe had taken a fearful beating. Even now it was showing signs of collapsing beneath them and it was unlikely that it could have withstood the punishment of a long haul to the coast. The seal of their fate was growing in the sky above them. A dark storm grew menacingly. The elements had not yet finished with them. This, Lyne knew, must be the end. Neither man had the energy to withstand much more.

Lyne and Thomas could feel the canoe rising higher and lower as the sea stirred then heaved, gathering a momentum that eventually broke into the crashing of waves. The storm was as fierce as it had been on the previous night. Acting now like automatons they dug in their blades to swing on to the waves. Their hands, savaged and torn by the beating, bled as they clutched the paddles. They could not keep this up much longer. Willmott had made it clear to them back at HMS *Dolphin* that there was a very good chance their mission might be one-way. These prophetic words were now becoming starkly true. The end would not be long now . . .

But the sea was not to have them. They had been spotted—by the enemy. An armed enemy trawler churned through the sea towards them. They saw it when it was too late to do anything other than sink the canoe with the thrust of a knife into the stabilising air bags. As the canoe sank beneath them the trawler drew alongside and they were hauled on board at gun point. Resistance was futile. They had only a revolver and it is doubtful if either of them would have had the strength to pull the trigger. Both of them collapsed and awoke in separate cells under French guard. When they had recovered they were separately interrogated but their cover stories appeared to be accepted as true. From then on, until the invasion came, they were treated like guests by their captors, who feasted them with good food and wine.

The invasion of French North Africa began on 7 November, 1942 amid turbulent seas. The foul weather encountered by the canoeists at Algiers had continued unabated and spread west to the other landing area around Oran. But at Oran at least the landing went without any appreciable hitch, aided on its way by the submarines and the markers' canoes. Algiers was quite a different story. There, complete chaos reigned. The weather was so bad that the canoes were, even from the outset, in danger of sinking but they heroically took up their positions where the canoes sat swamped in water and sent signals out to sea to guide in the attackers.

The confusion was caused by a last-minute change of plan when a hurried conference was called aboard the ship carrying the Senior Naval Officer (Landings). He proposed a delay in launching the assault craft and a bitter argument ensued during which the whole invasion fleet drifted wildly off course. The result of this found Willmott in a landing craft trying to rescue the remnants of wildly scattered boats and herd them into order before leading them ashore. Many were too far away to be rescued and landed on beaches miles away from their intended targets. Willmott did, however, succeed in getting those he had rounded up on to the right beach, despite a shore fog which shrouded it.

When dawn came, the shambles was there for all to see. Landing craft were strewn all along the coast. Tanks which had landed on beaches wholly unsuitable for them had transformed them into death-traps for vehicles following in their wake. One misguided beach master had ignored the aid offered by Willmott's navigator and led his assault craft ashore by himself—landing eight miles off target.

Later Willmott's pleas for a personal beach survey were vindicated when several landing craft ran aground on hidden sand bars which his men would have found in a survey. As a result, when the soldiers leapt off the craft into the sea, they landed in deep water. Fortunately the beach was not defended by the enemy, otherwise these soldiers could have been wiped out at a stroke.

Vehicles were landed on beaches with no exits and found themselves trapped and at the mercy of German dive bombers which plummeted out of the sky after dawn.

The only thing that saved the invasion force from total annihilation was the weak defences. Had they been stronger the outcome would have been too awful to contemplate. Many of the incidents that occurred that night could have been avoided had Willmott only been allowed to carry out a proper beach reconnaissance. But his superiors were taking a painfully and dangerously long time to recognise the sense of his suggestions. Perhaps, he hoped, the shambles of the North African invasion would change their minds. It did—and in a dramatic way.

Willmott was whisked back to England by air, and he had hardly alighted from the aeroplane before he was ordered to the headquarters of Combined Operations. Now the lesson had been learned and it won him droves of supporters in high and influential places. Willmott was ordered to form and command a unit to be trained and held in readiness for use in beach intelligence operations prior to future amphibious invasions. There were to be no half measures now. His new unit, to be known as Combined Operations Pilotage Parties, was to comprise no fewer than *fifty* teams.

Elated, Willmott sank himself into the complex business of directing the formation and training of COPP. Purpose-built canoes were supplied, specially-designed suits for beach parties were made, a rigid and rigorous fitness programme was devised and a vast array of equipment obtained, often by devious means. At a small yacht club on Hayling Island, the embryo COPP blossomed and when the reclamation of Europe began, with the invasion of Sicily, teams of Willmott's Coppists had already scouted the beaches.

The perils of the missions upon which these men embarked were never more forcibly highlighted than at Sicily. Here, four submarines launched fifteen men to scout the proposed landing beaches. Of that fifteen, five disappeared without trace, another five were captured and another two, who failed to rendezvous with their submarine, *paddled* the eighty miles back to their base at Malta. They were tough men—Willmott saw to that. And they knew that if they met their death upon these nocturnal operations, they would almost certainly die alone. This was a risk they willingly took.

There were to be more sacrifices as far afield as the Far East when the massed onslaught began upon the Japanese, but without doubt the great moment for COPP came with the D-day landings on the Normandy beaches. Braving the most heavily-defended shores in the whole of the Nazi fortress, Willmott and his men slipped on to the beaches, took samples from them, reconnoitred and returned home with their findings. And when the mightiest armada ever assembled charged towards the beaches on June 6, 1944, it was the Coppists who led them in. Lying offshore from the British and Canadian beaches were two midget submarines with Coppists on board who shone beacons out to sea to light the way in. The Americans, showing all the reluctance the Royal Navy had shown in the very beginning, declined the offer of Coppists to guide them in. The result was the slaughter of 3,000 men on 'Omaha' Beach where they had landed off target under the muzzles of heavy German guns. If only they had listened to Willmott, that massacre might well have been avoided.

But for the courage, foresight and determination of Lieutenant Commander Nigel Willmott, DSO, DSC and bar, RN, the greatest invasion in the history of Man might well have ended in disaster. The resilience shown by Willmott and his Coppists in undertaking what must rank among the most hazardous and secret operations of the war unquestionably helped in bringing an end to that awful conflict.

3

Terror from the Skies

Paul Josef Goebbels, Hitler's propaganda chief before and during the Second World War, was the media 'mouth' of Germany's Third Reich. A scholar and fanatical Nazi, he was perhaps the only important member of the Party hierarchy who could lay claim to a higher education.

A popular barrack room ballad of the time claimed that '. . . poor old Goebbels had no balls at all!' The veracity of that is questionable since the propaganda minister was a family man with children—all of whom he poisoned to death as Russian troops fought their way through the streets of Berlin towards Hitler's Chancellory in 1945.

Throughout the war years, Goebbels proved himself a master of the art of propaganda. He excelled in manipulating truths and half truths—exaggerating small military gains, transforming defeat into victory—and in downright, blatant lying. He was a bragger without peer and his rantings before the German people on platform, film and radio held the nation spellbound. His pen re-wrote crushing defeat into staggering victory for the German forces, even when 1,000 bomber raids on the Fatherland were clear evidence of his falsehoods.

Radio transmissions from the Reich clearly had the 'Goebbels touch'. And while the vast bulk of the news that filtered through the ether was manifestly false, it was from time to time punctuated with alarming truth. Alas, as is often the case when listening to persistent and·obvious liars, there is a tendency to disbelieve *all* they claim. As events were to prove, this was to be a dangerous belief—and one that might well have had catastrophic consequences for Britain, had it not been for a combination of luck, the courage of secret agents, the persistence of RAF Intelligence, and Allied bombers.

When Goebbels' Ministry of Information bragged of Germany's secret *Vergeltung* (revenge) weapons, this was no idle boast. British Intelligence put it down to typically alarmist propaganda. Perhaps they might have been justified, had it not been for a succession of hints and tip-offs from their own agents within German occupied countries.

The Second World War was barely a month old when a letter arrived on the desk of the British Military Attache´ in Oslo, Norway's capital. The Attache´ was puzzled by the contents of this note. It was unsigned and in plain language, offering to impart information to the British about the most up-to-date advances in German military technology. At first reading, the letter had the touch of a 'crank', some well-meaning, but misguided person who wished to help the Allies. The Attache´ was tempted to consign the letter to the waste paper basket, but instead he re-read it. Now another thought occurred to him. The letter might well have come from the German Secret Service. They were sufficiently wily to offer false information to mislead British Intelligence. Either of these two possibilities could be true—but on the other hand, the letter could be genuine. It pointed out that if the British wanted to take up the offer, then they were to change the introduction to the BBC broadcast in German on a particular night a few days later. Whatever the true intention of the writer, the Attache´ could see no harm in doing this and it was duly arranged.

On the appointed night, the BBC broadcast began '*Hullo! Hier ist London*'. This was the signal and the Attache´ waited to see what, if anything, would happen. He did not have long to wait. A lengthy document, again unsigned, arrived. It contained what appeared to be some quite staggering revelations. The list of top-secret projects was seemingly endless. It mentioned in detail that German scientists were perfecting radio range-finding equipment; two new types of radar, code-named *Würzburg* and *Freya*; a remote-controlled glider bomb; a radio beam navigational system code-named *Knickebein* for homing bombers on to their targets; rocket-propelled flying bombs and long-range supersonic ballistic rockets. These were a few of its revelations. It was a massive document, and its very size gave rise to suspicion as to its authenticity within the British Secret Intelligence Service. Clearly, if the contents of the letter were true, they could only have been sent by some leading scientist or high-ranking German. No-one else would have had such knowledge. On the other hand the whole document could be pure invention, concocted by the Germans themselves. Since neither letter was signed, and no hint was given as to the sender's identity, the British Intelligence Service decided to disbelieve the contents. As events were later to prove, every single item detailed in the 'Oslo report' was *true*. But who sent it? To this day that remains a mystery. There was some speculation that it was sent by none other than Admiral Wilhelm Canaris, head of the German Intelligence Service. He had a bitter hatred of Adolf Hitler and indeed was later executed for his part in a plot to assassinate the Führer. Was his determination to bring Hitler down so great that he would even go to the extent of revealing his country's most closely guarded secrets? It is doubtful if we will ever know. The author's identity is really only of academic importance. The tragedy was that the report, although not entirely ignored, was discounted as unreliable and imponderable, duly filed and all but forgotten. Some time later, a similar report came from a Danish agent. That too was filed.

As Hitler's army overran the countries of Europe, more intelligence filtered through to London. Warning whispers came from every corner of Nazi-dominated Europe but they lacked concrete evidence, something tangible that would prove beyond doubt the existence of, or experimentation in, these terror weapons.

The truth was that Germany was indeed well advanced in the development of *Wunderwaffen*—the V-1 flying bomb and its even more devastating big brother, the V-2 rocket. Since the 1920s scientists had been working on the pulse jet engine which would propel a pilotless aircraft containing high explosives on to a target. The concept of bombarding an enemy's cities, industrial complexes and strong points with rockets and flying bombs from within Germany or her occupied countries meant that, in theory at least, she could carry on a war with impunity. The V-1 bomb was the first of these weapons to become a working reality when, in 1942, it had reached the prototype stage and was ready for test firing.

The flying bomb that evolved from years of experimentation was cigar-shaped with short, stubby main wings set amidships on the fuselage and a lateral pair of even shorter wings at the tail. The propulsion unit which housed the pulse jet was contained within a long tube mounted above the tail. The complete bomb weighed a little over two tons, being constructed in the main of pressed steel. It was 25.4 feet in length with a wing span of 17.7 feet. The motor was a single Argus pulse jet engine, which developed a thrust of 740 pounds, giving the bomb a cruising speed of around 400 miles an hour at a height of 3,000 feet.

The bomb had many advantages, not the least of which was its operating height. Flying at 3,000 feet, it was too low and fast to be shot down by the heavy anti-aircraft guns, which were most effective against high-flying targets, and too high to be hit by the light anti-aircraft guns.

It was Hitler's intention to rain *one thousand* of these bombs down upon Britain *every day*, beginning in December 1943. The prospect of such a fate for Britain was awful enough but if the V-2 wingless rocket which was supersonic and more powerful than the flying bomb were to fall on Britain in great numbers, the result would have been too terrible to contemplate, for the V-2 was unstoppable. There was little doubt that Germany could bring Britain to her knees without a single German stepping on British soil—and this dreadful prospect remained, if not totally unknown, unheeded by British Intelligence.

The first real fears of the existence of these weapons were felt with a report from the Polish Underground. Following the German occupation of Poland, it became the practice to send young Poles to forced labour work in Germany as part of the Germanisation process. The Germans imagined that by doing this, they could mould the Poles into Germanic thought and action. Young men of all classes were transported to many parts of the Reich, generally to undertake menial tasks on farms and industrial sites. What the Germans failed to appreciate was that, in doing so, they were aiding a very active Polish Underground Movement by sending its agents far afield where they could gather information that could be used against the Reich.

Some of those first warning elbow nudges of a flying bomb menace came from a Pole deported to the island of Usedom lying at the mouth of the River Oder in the Western Baltic. It was to part of the island known as Peenemünde that a young Polish teacher was sent for his period of forced labour. Typical of his new masters, they made no use of his professional talents, perhaps fearing that, as a Pole and a teacher, he might persuade his scholars against the 'master race'. Doubtless, these fears were justified, for the young Pole was a patriot with a bitter hatred of the Nazi hordes which had invaded his country, but the decision to deport him to Peenemünde was to be one of the Germans' greatest mistakes of the war. He was put to work constructing roads and gun emplacements. His work did not, however, take him into a top secret, heavily guarded area which housed an airfield and some unusual concrete constructions, all hidden behind a dense barrier of trees.

The unseen activities within that security area excited the Pole's interest. Days and nights were interrupted by deafening roars the like of which he had never heard before. His curiosity knew no bounds but try as he might, he could glean no information about what went on in the secret site. Speculation was rife among his fellow workers but no one could throw any light on the mystery. Then, one day, the Polish teacher and a fellow worker were ordered off their normal duties and detailed to go into the top-secret site at Peenemünde to clean out toilets and washrooms. This was to prove a profound error of judgement on the part of the Germans.

One morning, while the two Poles were pushing a barrow-load of waste to the incinerator they happened to pass a large shed. The big sliding doors to this building had always been securely locked every time the Poles had passed it before but on this particular day, it was slightly ajar and a light shone inside. A quick glance revealed that there were no Germans around. This gave the teacher the opportunity he had been waiting for. While his friend kept a look-out, the teacher sidled over to the half-opened door and peered inside. The sight that met his eyes brought a frown to his brow. He just could not understand what he saw. Standing on trestles in the centre of the shed was a strange aircraft. It was smaller than anything he had ever seen before and there were two features that struck him as odd. There was no cockpit for a pilot and stranger still, no propeller. The teacher was puzzled but there was no time to contemplate further . . .

A sharp warning whistle from his friend brought the teacher darting back to the barrow as the crunch of jackboots heralded the approach of a German soldier. The two Poles went on about their business but now their minds were abuzz with the thoughts of what their find might be. Two factors were blatantly obvious: the teacher had never seen an aircraft like that one before and the

Germans were going to extraordinary lengths to keep it secret. There was absolutely no doubt that their discovery would be of interest to the Underground in Poland. Within a few days the information had percolated through an intricate network of agents and into Poland from where it was relayed to England. Another piece of an intriguing jigsaw arrived at British Intelligence but the tragedy was that no-one had seriously begun to piece that jigsaw puzzle together.

What in fact the Polish teacher had unwittingly discovered was the focal point of German rocket research, a £50,000,000 complex where Germany's top scientists were working day and night in the perfection of the terror weapons. Here and throughout many German occupied countries some 40,000 people were at work building up the massive new arsenal of flying bombs and rockets. Successful firings of both flying bombs and rockets took place towards the end of 1942. But even before then, the intense preparations underway at Peenemünde had been 'seen' by the RAF's Photo Intelligence Service—and filed for future reference! A photograph which showed that some unusual work was underway at Peenemünde was taken quite by chance and lay in a box along with many others at the headquarters of the Photographic Interpretation Unit at RAF Station, Medmenham.

RAF Medmenham was no fighter or bomber base, but a quiet tudor-style mansion which lay near the Thames between Henley and Marlow. Within its walls was housed the PIU which was responsible for the interpretation of photographs brought back to England by photo-reconnaissance aircraft. Thousands of photographs were scrutinised by experts whose job it was to get from these prints even the most minute scrap of information which might be of military importance.

In a small room there was one young WAAF officer who was destined to play a leading role in revealing the menace that lay on that Baltic island of Usedom. She was Constance Babington-Smith. Through her hands passed countless photographs of enemy territory. She scrutinised every one, scouring them through a stereoscope, for anything that might prove useful. She and her team were to uncover some truly remarkable secrets by their skill and diligence but perhaps the most amazing of all was the discovery that the Germans' claims to having terror weapons was no idle boast.

Reconnaissance flights over enemy territory by specially equipped aircraft of the RAF were an everyday occurrence. A variety of aircraft was used but the most successful were the Spitfire and later the Mosquito. They were fast and carried no armament. Their guns were replaced by cameras. If they got into a tangle with the enemy, they had to rely upon their superior speed and manoeuvrability to get them out of trouble. These two elements were their sole defence. The courage displayed by their crews was immense. They flew when the sky was clear—the very time when they were most likely to be spotted by the enemy. Clear skies meant no cloud to dodge into if trouble loomed. Theirs was a precarious adventure and one they undertook with signal courage. Not for them the accolades accorded their counterparts in the fighter and bomber squadrons. These 'spies in the sky', like those who worked secretly on the ground, seldom sought or received any award for their work. It was men like these who provided Babington-Smith and her teams with the miles of film and thousands of prints from which they could uncover enemy strength or predict enemy intentions.

One such pilot was Flight Lieutenant D. W. Steventon. On 15 May, 1942, his Spitfire shot across the western shores of the Baltic. His cameras had already captured the latent images of units of the German fleet at the port of Kiel. Now he nosed his aircraft along a course for Swinemünde to photograph reported movements of enemy shipping there. As the Spitfire darted across the sky for the port, Steventon's eyes swept the coastline beneath him. He caught sight of the island of Usedom and at its tip an airfield. Near the complex of runways were some constructional workings. Speed of decision was a vital element in the make-up of the photo-reconnaissance pilot. Hesitation meant opportunities lost but Steventon did not miss this chance.

A deft flick of the control column brought the Spitfire sweeping over to cross the island. Steventon switched on his cameras and bolted across the fan-shaped tip of land, known as Peenemünde. The shutters blinked, arresting the scene below on film. Then the run was over in a fraction of a minute and the Spitfire winged its way on towards Swinemünde.

Later that day, the Spitfire landed back in England. The reels of film were processed and printed then rushed to the Photo Interpretation Unit at Medmenham. The prints came under the eagle eyes of several specialists then were passed on to Babington-Smith. It was she who noticed something unusual nearby the airfield; a series of 'mysterious rings' apparently built of concrete. But neither she nor anyone else at the PIU could figure out what they were or were intended for. The series of photographs taken by Steventon was therefore filed for future reference—it was to be seven months before they were referred to again. The PIU had found a vital clue to what was going on at Peenemünde but the link between Hitler's *Vergeltungswaffen* (revenge weapons) and these concrete circles had not been appreciated. That was to come later.

In the last three months of 1942, the first successful launchings of both the V-1 and the V-2 took place. This success was the signal for an all-out effort in preparing the vital launching sites from which a second blitz of England would begin. Even this was not to escape the notice of agents. They were not spies in the sky but courageous agents on the ground who risked hazards even greater than those of their counterparts in the air. One such man led the field in bringing to light one of Germany's most closely kept secrets. He did so, not so much by subterfuge and undercover work but by seemingly blatant—and dangerous—collaboration with the enemy. Through this man's daring, the 'red light' flashed at the headquarters of British Intelligence; another segment of the growing jigsaw was to fit into place and point to the impending Armageddon.

The true identity of 'Robin', as this agent was known, is still a closely guarded secret. He, like many of those who worked for the Allies within enemy territory throughout the war, prefers to maintain his anonimity. Robin was an amateur spy, but only in the sense that he never received any payment for his considerable services as a spy—indeed quite the opposite. He was a wealthy businessman, born in Switzerland and educated in France, where he built up a very substantial international business. When war came, Robin financed his espionage and sabotage very largely out of his own pocket.

France fell to the Germans in 1940 and it would have been a simple matter for 'Robin' to flee the country, return to his neutral birth-place of Switzerland or indeed any other safe country, taking his fortune with him and continuing business. There were two very good reasons why this would have been a very sensible move for the wealthy Swiss; firstly he was a fervent anti-Nazi but even more importantly, he was a Jew. Hitler's persecution of the Jews was well known. The concentration camp and subsequent elimination were almost certainties for any Jew in a Nazi occupied country. Robin would have been a natural target and a candidate for the gas chamber which was designed to solve the 'Jewish problem'. But despite the danger he resolved to stay in Paris and fight.

Robin had the advantage of not looking Jewish. He was tall, fair haired and had striking blue eyes. Indeed his appearance seemed to conform more to Hitler's idea of the ideal Aryan than that of a Jew, the object of his manifest hatred.

When the Wehrmacht marched into Paris and the French government capitulated, Robin saw his opportunity of helping the Allies. High ranking and privileged Germans, among them many Nazis, frequented the exclusive hotels and restaurants which were the haunts of the wealthy Swiss and well within his financial means. He dined alongside the élite of the occupation forces, both military and civilian. While doing so, it did not escape him that if he could cultivate the friendship of some of the Germans he rubbed shoulders with, he might get information that could be useful to London. He was a regular visitor to all the best restaurants, hotels and night clubs in Paris. He spoke fluent German and as an accomplished negotiator in international business, found no difficulty in infiltrating the social circles of the Germans who helped themselves to the very best that Paris could 'offer'. Robin posed as a pro-Nazi Alsatian businessman by the name of Jacques Walter. His command of the German language, 'pro-German sympathies', Aryan looks and wealth made him a welcome addition to the German social round. Although in his early forties, Robin was still a bachelor and led a high life, doing the rounds of the night clubs, seeking out those Germans whom he reckoned would be useful to him. But while 'Herr Walter' outwardly tasted of life's rich fruits, he was engaged in clandestine operations. He had been well connected in France before the war and now he put these contacts to good use. One friend of his was a member of the Secret Service in France and through him, Robin was put in contact with the British Secret Intelligence Service. He was embraced with open arms. Robin was just the sort of agent the British were looking for. One night he was missing from his usual haunts in Paris. He had another engagement. His 'date' for that night was not a nubile young mademoiselle but a group of officers on board a Royal Navy motor torpedo boat. Robin was urged to cultivate his friendships with the Germans and supplied with contacts through whom he could get in touch with London. With that he returned to Paris.

Throughout the months that followed, Robin filtered snatches of information through to England and he soon established himself as one of the most important spies in France. But, not content with simple espionage, he became restive for real action and was recruited by another secret British organisation, the Special Operations Executive, whose agents engaged in sabotage in the German-occupied countries. Here too Robin played a major role.

By now, the German anti-Jewish net had spread to France and Semitic Frenchmen, women and children were being rounded up and transported to concentration camps for extermination. Robin could not stand by and watch the mass deportation of his kin. He determined to use what influence he could to save some of these poor wretches from the gas chamber.

The slightest hint of Jewish ancestry was sufficient to condemn a person to death—even if he did not practise his faith or was several generations removed from those who had. Such people were the Sephardics. They made up a community of people who were the descendents of Portuguese and Spanish Jews who had fled to France during the Spanish Inquisition. Very few of them practised the Jewish religion but their remotely tenuous link with Judaism was sufficient to earmark them for deportation. Robin was acquainted with their leader who implored him to try and persuade his German 'friends' to exclude the community from deportation. Robin promised to do what he could, but he did not hold out much hope.

It happened that Robin knew a certain Captain Dannecker who was based in Paris and was on the staff of Obersturmbanführer Eichmann, the man responsible for the mass execution of the Jews. Dannecker was Eichmann's Paris representative and as such played a leading role in the selection of those for deportation. He was to be Robin's target.

Robin found it difficult to contain himself in the presence of the vile creature with whom he set about negotiating the salvation of the Sephardic community. This cretinous Nazi was the manifestation of all that Robin hated. The stroke of Dannecker's pen or the nod of his head was enough to pronounce the death sentence. He was judge and jury in the trial of thousands of French Jews. But Robin had to restrain himself. These negotiations were delicate and he dared not appear too anxious in his bid to save those he *professed* to hate, otherwise it might give rise to suspicion.

He knew that there was one temptation that might turn Dannecker's head—the promise of substantial sums of money. 'Herr Walter' pointed out to Dannecker and his equally evil henchmen that the Sephardic community was a rich one, willing to pay handsomely for the favour of being overlooked. At that the posse of persecutioners began to bend towards Robin's arguments in favour of the Sephardics. When the spy offered to deposit the sum of one million dollars in a Swiss bank account, the deal seemed clinched. It was agreed that the entire Sephardic community could remain in France as ordinary Frenchmen and their papers would make no reference to their Jewish ancestry. Robin was delighted—but his elation was short-lived. Someone 'squealed' to the SD, the Nazi *Sicherheitsdienst*, or Secret Police. That brought the negotiations to an abrupt end. Robin could do no more. The SD was beyond corruption. They never struck bargains.

Had it not been for Robin's careful and professional skill in handling the abortive affair as well as his professed pro-Nazi sympathies, he might have been exposed. He dared not have the SD delving too deply into his background. But by then, the summer of 1942, he had become such an accepted part of the German scene in Paris that he escaped suspicion and was able to continue his spy work unhindered.

The gay social whirl of parties continued during which Robin struck up more and important friendships with the élite of the occupation forces. It was about that time that, several hundred miles away, at Peenemünde, the Germans were making their first successful launches of the V-1 and V-2 rockets that Robin made what was probably his most fruitful conquest of the war.

The meeting took place at a party which fairly sparkled with the gold braid of senior German officers. Generals abounded amid the mass of people enjoying the finest of France's wines and food at the cocktail party held in the sumptuous surroundings of a plush Paris house, near the notorious Avenue Foch; 'notorious' because it housed the headquarters of the Gestapo whose brutality was well known. But the two houses might well have been poles apart. While the most heinous of crimes were being committed in the Avenue Foch, the gaiety of the party nearby knew no bounds. Champagne flowed freely and the atmosphere was heady with the riches consumed by the 'conquerors'.

Robin 'circulated' among the groups of Germans, Frenchmen and their ladies, as was the custom on these occasions. The clinking of glasses and bursts of laughter were punctuated by the inevitable heel clicking as introductions were made. Robin detected several new faces among the revellers but one attracted his special attention, because he stood alone. Typical of his type he was overweight, with a thick bull neck and close-cropped hair. He might have fitted the description of many Germans had it not been for the obviously expensive cut of his suit of civilian clothes. This little man interested Robin and he resolved to meet him.

Robin shouldered his way through the throng until he 'cornered' his hostess. She was a lady well known in Paris society who knew Robin of old and was well aware that he was not the Jacques Walter he claimed to be. However, she knew nothing of his clandestine activities but realised that there must be a very good reason for his wishing to remain incognito. Her guest asked if she might arrange for him to meet the corpulent German and she readily agreed without questioning his motive. Together they made their way to the little man who, although well filled with vintage champagne, seemed out of the swing of things and clearly keen to join in but finding it difficult to do so.

The introduction was duly made and Robin clasped the German's podgy hand as names were exchanged, Robin as 'Herr Walter' and the German as a 'Herr Professor—' whose name was lost in the babble of chatter around them. Robin immediately engaged the German in conversation and quickly learned that the newcomer was a representative of no less a personage than Reichsminister Speer, Hitler's Minister of Production and Munitions. Robin could hardly believe his good fortune. Speer's ministry was the one that made the German war machine 'tick' and if the professor was a member of his staff—and a senior one at that—he could be a veritable mine of information.

Robin realised that he would have to treat this new find with considerable subtlety. The professor was no fool, and unlikely to let information slip. He was also careful to steer the conversation away from his job and the war. Robin knew that he was going to be a tough nut to crack. There must, he thought, be some way of getting at him, some flaw in his armour—and he found it. The German had a penchant for the ladies and was a heavy drinker. New to Paris, he was eager to taste its fruits and he begged Robin to be his escort around the night spots. The spy willingly agreed and suggested that there was no time like the present. When they left the party together, the German was already the worse for liquor. But the night was young and Robin promised him a night he would never forget. There began a Bacchic binge which lasted the remainder of the night and gave the professor his first real taste of the delights of Paris. The pub crawl was made somewhat easier since they were transported in a large SS staff car. The chauffeur-driven car served to reinforce Robin's conviction that he had found a very high ranking drinking companion.

The German's eyes bulged out of his fat head at the sight of the naked dancers in the cabarets of the Champs Elysées and Robin toyed with the idea of introducing him to a young 'lady friend'. Robin had plenty of these whom he knew he could trust but since it was a commonly accepted fact that women do not make good spies, especially where technical information was concerned, he decided to handle this man on his own. Dawn was almost upon Paris when the night of drinking finally came to an end and the professor, hardly able to stand, retired to his hotel, the Royal Monceau. But before parting company with Robin, he made him promise that they would have another such night the following night. The spy could not have been happier and said he would call for him.

Everything Robin had seen that evening pointed to the professor being in the upper echelon of Speer's staff. He would have to be given the 'kid glove' treatment. The slightest possible slip might betray Robin's true identity and intent and he realised that the fewer people who knew of his new acquaintance, the safer the secret would be. So he told no one, not even his closest collaborators in the Underground. Not a whisper of the relationship left Robin's lips—not even to London. Only if he got something of interest would the silence be broken. Until then he braced himself for the booze-up of a lifetime. But there was to be a shock in store for the spy at his next meeting with the Herr

Professor . . .

The following night, Robin obediently presented himself at the Royal Monceau Hotel and was shown to the professor's elegant suite on the fourth floor. But when he entered, it took him a moment to recognise his drinking friend of the previous night. The German was in the uniform of a Standartenführer, a brigadier, of the élite SS. Robin showed his surprise and his friend was quick to notice the puzzled look. He gave a chuckle and apologised for his formal appearance. The German explained that, although he was a professor of civil engineering, in his ministerial capacity he held the rank of Standartenführer and was obliged to wear his uniform when undertaking official duties.

After the professor had made a quick change into civilian clothes, the two left the Monceau, again in the chauffeur-driven car, and embarked upon a king-size night on the town. The German's appetite for drink and girls knew no bounds and it was not long before he was reeling under the excesses of both. Wobbling on his unsteady legs, he was helped out of the last cabaret and into the car. It was clear that he could take no more—nor indeed could Robin who, throughout the night, had had to resort to some surreptitious sleight-of-hand with the brim-full glasses of wine and cognac to avoid getting too drunk himself. He knew that if he became too intoxicated, he would be unable to wrest any worthwhile information out of the German. As it was, his brain was dulled by the amount of alcohol he had consumed.

Robin decanted the Standartenführer into the car and they were driven back to the Monceau. It took both Robin and the chauffeur to 'un-cork' the heavy German from his drunken half-sleep in the back of the car but once outside, Robin insisted that he should help his friend back to his suite. He told a grateful chauffeur that he could go.

While the paralytic German muttered slurred words of thanks to Robin he was navigated up to his suite. Robin was exhausted after the struggle to get the heavyweight upstairs but he knew that it was now that the real work would begin. He had to concentrate, despite his fuzzy brain. Wobbling under the weight of the podgy Prussian, Robin staggered over to the bed and dropped his companion on to it. He was already dead to the world so Robin undressed him and left him to sleep. Now was the opportunity he had been waiting for, the chance to have a look around the suite.

He made his way through to the sumptuous sitting room next door to a solo performance of sonorous snores from the bedroom. Robin soon found what he had been looking for—the inevitable briefcase. The Germans had what amounted to a fetish about briefcases, as if they were some sort of status symbol. The Standartenführer was no exception. There it was on the writing desk, and it was unlocked. Robin took a quick look at the recumbent German just to confirm that he was still asleep, then quickly returned to the briefcase. He gaped in almost disbelief when he withdrew the wodge of papers from it. Many of them were of no interest but some were clearly marked secret. They referred to a variety of engineering projects, some already under way and others planned for the future.

Robin had to restrain a gasp as he carefully examined each document, sifting through them and committing to memory morsels of information that looked as if they might be of interest to London. He couldn't believe his luck. Here he had a man who dealt in top secret projects and was careless enough to leave them in an unlocked briefcase. What a find. But he dared not press his luck too far. He replaced the documents with infinite care, ensuring that they were put back exactly as he had found them. Back in the bedroom, he gave the unconscious professor a smile of 'gratitude', then left.

The following day the salient points he had extracted from the documents were transmitted to London. News of the projects would doubtless find its way to the RAF and in due course receive the attention of Bomber Command.

Night after night, Robin and the Standartenführer did the rounds of the bars. They were by now 'bosom friends'. And each tour of the high spots of Paris ended with the German being tucked in for the night by Robin who then took advantage of the professor's drunken stupor to glean more secrets from the briefcase. The result was an upsurge in sabotage of key German installations and, for the Germans, a baffling increase in the accuracy of the RAF's bombing. The German intelligence services were baffled. There was clearly a leak of vital information but they could not pin-point where it came from.

In London the accuracy of Robin's reports was received with amazement but there were even greater things to come. As the nights of revelry continued the Standartenführer took Robin more and more into his confidence. Until then the German had, even when he was the worse for drink, avoided discussing the subject of war and its progress. But now he took to talking about it more readily. He showed particular concern for the turn of events in the war in North Africa and was clearly worried. Robin sensed that his friend had inside information that had given rise to this mood of concern. His suspicions were to be proved correct. Robin made an all out effort one night early in October 1942, to get the German totally paralytic through drink so that he could devote more attention to the papers in the briefcase. Robin drowned his unsuspecting companion in choice vintage and it had the desired effect.

By now, Robin was well known at the Royal Monceau Hotel. To the night porter the sight of him assisting the Standartenführer to his suite was commonplace and aroused no comment. On this particular night—or rather morning, for it was almost dawn—Robin went through the usual routine. Reeling from the effects of liquor the German quickly fell into a drunken sleep and Robin made straight for the all-important briefcase. He soon found what he had been looking for. It was in the form of a directive from Speer himself, ordering the Standartenführer to ensure that certain spare parts for tanks which were being manufactured in France were ready for shipment to North Africa by convoy from Brindisi to Benghazi on October 20. These spare parts were vital to the German General Rommel's panzer tanks. Without them, the Afrika Korps might well grind to a halt. The directive indicated that the convoy would also be carrying supplies of petrol, equally important to Rommel. This was without doubt the juiciest piece of information that Robin had discovered so far. He lost no time in passing it on to London.

In due course, RAF aircraft massed for an all-out onslaught upon the convoy which set sail just as Robin had predicted. Between 26 and 28 October, the RAF rained hell and damnation down upon it with the result that three tankers were sunk. The epic battle of El Alamein launched against Rommel's army by the British 8th Army under the command of General Montgomery had already begun. It swayed one way then the other, but lack of crucial supplies of fuel proved one of the decisive factors which forced Rommel into retreat and resulted some months later in the total surrender of the Afrika Korps. Had Robin's warning not come when it did, then the struggle in North Africa might have been a more protracted and bloody affair.

In the meantime, the Standartenführer continued to revel in the high life of Paris, completely unaware of Robin's duplicity. News of Rommel's reversals of fortune in the desert were the talk of Paris and came up in Robin's conversations with the German. But to Robin's surprise, the German seemed unperturbed, 'reassuring' him that he had no cause to worry, for the Reich had up its sleeve weapons that would change the course of the war in a very short time. He revealed that he had just had confirmation of the successful trials of the new weapons direct from Berlin. Immediately, Robin thought of the briefcase and wondered what startling revelations it might include. But his hopes of getting clues from there were dashed when the German added that the project was so secret that he had to carry the communiqué on his person at all times. This came as a blow to the spy, especially when, on that particular evening, the Standartenführer had begun the binge resplendent in his SS uniform. Clearly, the all-important document was in one of his pockets and that would make it all the more difficult for Robin to get at it—if he could do it at all.

Perhaps it was the news of the new weapons and the reassurance that all would be well that prompted the German to consume even more drink that night but whatever the reason, he went at it with a vengeance—so much so that he was sick. This was another set-back for Robin because he knew that the German might now sober up more quickly and wreck his chances of getting at the letter. His heart sank, for it meant that he would have to continue drinking and his consumption of wine and spirits had already left him woozy. But his determination to unveil the secret of the letter drove him on and he plied his companion with the most potent beverages he could find. Dawn came before Robin was satisfied that the German was sufficiently intoxicated and they returned to the hotel, then weaved a giddy path to the suite. Then came another setback. When Robin deposited him upon the bed, the Standartenführer momentarily came to and protested when Robin tried to divest him of his tunic. Some subconscious force overrode the power of the alcohol and reminded him of the letter. His head spinning, he told Robin he would sleep in his uniform. Then he seemed to lapse into a sleep—but an uneasy one. Perhaps he was suspicious; perhaps some inner voice was telling him to beware of 'Herr Walter'.

It was some time before Robin assured himself that the German had finally escaped into drunken oblivion and he carefully unbuttoned one of the top pockets of the sleeping man's tunic. But as Robin's fingers found the letter, the German rolled over, almost bringing Robin down on top of him. His hand was trapped. He risked a tug at the paper. The German stirred again. Robin stopped, the beads of cold sweat trickling down his forehead. He hardly dared breathe. But luck was with him. Robin pulled again until finally the letter was free. He slipped into the room next door, opened the envelope and extracted the folded document. Emblazoned upon it was the warning that the contents were top secret, so secret that they were to be seen by only the highest authorities. Robin began to translate. He was to uncover a pointer to one of the most closely guarded secrets of the war.

The contents of the letter referred to 'the success of the experiments in two secret projects at Peenemünde' and went on to say that 'the Führer has ordered preparations to be made to undertake constructional work of the heaviest nature in the coastal regions of Northern France.'*

Robin was baffled. He had never heard of Peenemünde and wondered what the two secret projects could be. With growing excitement, he read on.

The letter pointed out that the constructions would have to be in the form of shelters, with concrete roofs and walls like submarine pens. No firm date was set for the beginning of construction. This would follow when further tests had been completed at Peenemünde, but preparatory work had to begin at once so that '. . . the top secret construction work can begin the moment the Führer gives the order'.

The connection between the 'top secret projects' at Peenemünde and the 'heavy construction work' to be undertaken in Northern France baffled Robin, but of one thing he was quite certain: he'd hit upon something that he must get off to London as quickly as possible.

Robin returned to the bedroom and slipped the letter back into the German's pocket, then left. The following day this priceless information was transmitted to London. Robin had provided the

* From 'The World's Greatest Spies', by Charles Wighton, published by Odhams Press, 1962.

key to the door behind which lay one of the critical link pieces in the *Wunderwaffen* puzzle.

The murmurs of menace were growing in a crescendo to cries of dire warning. Although Robin knew nothing of Peenemünde, British Intelligence did. The pieces of information were amassed, the 'Oslo report' retrieved and the dust swept from it. Reports were scrutinised and the link between Hitler's *Vergeltungswaffen* and the 'heavy construction work' proposed for northern France was established. The Oslo report, the Polish teacher's discovery, the Danish message, Robin's brilliant piece of espionage and other fragments were pieced together, bringing the full horrific prospect into focus. The reports manifestly suggested a second blitz launched from France against southern England. But still the question remained—how? Theories abounded, ranging from long range guns to the truth: flying bombs and rockets. But even with all that intelligence amassed, there was still no positive proof of what lay in store. Hints, tip-offs, warnings there were a-plenty, but no-one in London had actually seen one of these *Wunderwaffen*—not even a drawing. An urgent call went out for more facts. Agents in all the German-occupied countries were alerted.

Meanwhile Robin, who had played such a magnificent part in unveiling the Germans' intent was about to lose his source of information. Only two days after he had made his remarkable discovery the Standartenführer was called to northern France. They were never to meet again. It is perhaps as well that their 'friendship' did end there, for Robin suspected that the German Secret Service had got wind of him and were poised to pounce. Herr 'Jacques Walter', the business man from Strasbourg prudently faded into the background.*

The warning that 'long range attacks' might come reached RAF Medmenham in February 1943. It was than that the unusual work being carried out at Peenemünde was remembered. Further reconnaissance sorties were flown over the secret German base and they revealed more workings in the shape of cir-

---

* Robin shed the guise of the businessman but continued his work of espionage and sabotage contributing in no small measure to the chaos caused for the Germans in France. Already a top spy, he became one of the greatest saboteurs in the French Resistance. In 1943, he got word that the SD were on to him and discovery was only a hair's breadth away. He escaped to Switzerland from where he continued his espionage activities until he was arrested by the Swiss authorities for contravening his country's neutrality. He was tried and found guilty. When the war ended, he was decorated by the British for his work. He later returned to Paris and set up business once more.

cular earth banks. This discovery caused some confusion. From the intelligence so far obtained, it was estimated that the German secret weapons would have to be launched from inclined ramps placed strategically along the north coast of France. The circular banks and the theory of the ramps just did not match up. Something was still missing and there were those in London who believed that the threat of a rocket bombardment was a gigantic Nazi hoax. It was not until all the evidence, ranging from the reconnaissance photographs to the agents reports, was presented to the chiefs of staff that the awful truth was fully appreciated by some for the first time. At long last, the threat was beginning to be taken seriously. Churchill appointed Duncan Sandys, at that time Joint Parliamentary Secretary to the Ministry of Supply, to mastermind a searching investigation into the secret weapons and evaluate the measure of the menace.

Aircraft of British and American reconnaissance squadrons photographed both Peenemünde and miles of North France and at Medmenham every print was searched for vital clues—but nothing absolutely conclusive came from these sorties. Exploration of the photographs in the minutest detail revealed nothing Intelligence did not already know. Such was the intensity of the reconnaissance flights that the law of averages alone was almost bound to play into the hands of Babington-Smith and her colleagues. Surely they must get a break. The greatest obstacle was that no one seemed to know exactly what they were looking for. In her book *Evidence in Camera*'* she points out just how vague the Air Ministry's instructions had been. She and her companions were asked to look out for '. . . three things; a long range gun, a remotely controlled rocket aircraft and some sort of tube located in a disused mine out of which a rocket could be squirted.' This pointed to the uncertainty felt at the Air Ministry as to just what the 'ace' was that the Germans had up their sleeves and highlighted the unbelievably difficult task facing the Photographic Interpretation Unit. The investigations reached fever pitch and PIU personnel worked day and night. Attention was particularly focused upon Peenemünde and one theory put forward was that the curious earthworks sited near the airfield on the island might be the launching pads for rockets.

* Published by David & Charles, 1974.

In May, Sandys, armed with an ever-growing dossier of intelligence, re-affirmed the belief that the search should be for a remotely controlled pilotless aircraft as well as ballistic rockets. Scrutineers were not looking for *one* revenge weapon—but at least *two*. The element of most critical importance at this stage was positively to determine just exactly what it was that Britain would be up against when Hitler unleashed his *Vergeltungswaffen*. The major breakthrough was at hand.

Photo-reconnaissance of Peenemünde was intensified and in June stepped up to an all time high. On the 2nd of that month photographs showed a huge upright column about 40 feet tall. Speculation now became nearer to certainty—it was the launching platform for a rocket. But one of them had yet to be seen. That bright summer month was to be the turning point. On the 23rd, Flight Sergeant E. P. H. Peek, overflew Peenemünde in a twin-engined photo-reconnaissance Mosquito. The island was bathed in sunshine and the photographs that resulted from that flight were crisp and clear. One of them was to expose part of the Nazi secret with startling clarity. Within one of the wide, round earthworks at Peenemünde, lying by a tall tower, were two vehicles with long trailers behind each of them. Lying on each trailer were two rockets—V-2s. Now, at long last, after four years of blind fumbling in a morass of morsels of intelligence the British Secret Service had positive photographic evidence which showed that Germany had a ballistic missile. Its range, how it was propelled, how devastating it would be, and when the first barrage would begin, were to be discovered later. These were crucial questions which had to be answered if Britain were to put up any defence against them.

The discovery of the V-2s at Peenemünde confirmed that the Germans did have a rocket, but what of the reported remotely controlled pilotless aircraft, the much smaller missile that the Polish teacher had seen and had been mentioned in the now all-important Oslo Report? Clear evidence of the existence of the V-1 flying bomb had yet to come. There were still those among the hierarchy of British scientists who were doubtful of its existence. They wanted photographic evidence. But the days passed and there were no signs of the elusive V-1. It would come—but not yet awhile.

It was here that Robin briefly re-entered the scene. Warned by

London to be on the watch for anything out of the ordinary by way of new construction work near the French coast, he passed the word around his group of agents. One of them struck gold close by the village of Watten, near Calais, when he became aware of intense forest clearing. To the casual observer this might have meant nothing, but to the trained agent it was worth reporting. News of this filtered through to PIU where it was discovered that that area had already been photographed sometime earlier by a reconnaissance flight. Another flight over Watten produced photographs showing that a great deal of heavy construction work had been carried out in the intervening time. This was it—the beginning of the work to provide the launching sites for the missiles that were to bombard the south of England.

Those in power in London now had enough evidence to take some positive action to thwart Hitler's progress in the development of the V-weapons. The decision was taken to launch a 570-strong bomber raid on Peenemünde. On the night of 17/18 August, 1943, 571 bombers took off from England and set course as if they were to attack Berlin. It was an attempt to fool the Germans into thinking that the attack was to be against their capital. But the bomber stream changed course and thundered over Peenemünde. Bomb doors opened, exposing the clusters of high-explosive bombs in the bellies of the aircraft, then they rained down upon the rocket development site. In the hell that ensued more than 700 people were killed, among them some of the top rocket scientists, and buildings housing precious plans, equipment, stores and the fruits of years of scientific labour were destroyed. Over 1,000 tons of bombs which had saturated the experimental area all but devastated Peenemünde but forty-one British aircraft were lost. Subsequent reconnaissance photographs showed the area pock-marked by hundreds of bomb craters, buildings now heaps of rubble. Estimates of the effect that this raid had upon the development of the V weapons vary considerably but it is generally agreed that development of the flying bomb was delayed by about six months and the V-2 rocket by a year. Had the attack not taken place, the course of the war might have been quite different. Because of the raid, General Dornberger, head of the development plant at Peenemünde, was forced to move V-2 development elsewhere—out of the range of British bombers and 'safe' from discovery and attack. As we shall see, there was to be no safe hiding place.

To add further to the delay of the second Blitz, the USAAF launched a bomber raid upon the mysterious constructions at Watten, near Calais, in northern France. Dornberger later admitted that the raids could not have been better timed to cause temporary chaos. The Watten site was intended as a launching point for the V-2s but was now a tangled mass of rubble. It was easier to start again from the beginning.

The Germans were nothing if they were not resolute. Peenemünde and Watten may have been transformed into giant heaps of rubble but there was other secret work afoot, other developments planned, and already work had begun on them in preparation for the onslaught which Hitler was determined to unleash against England. Again, it was in France that a discovery was made that was to jolt the Allies once more—and it was a Frenchman who made it.

Michel Hollard was a spy—a self-appointed agent who, like Robin, had become involved in espionage upon his own initiative. But unlike Robin, Hollard was no rich businessman. He was small in stature but well built and in his early forties when France was overrun by the invading Germans. Hollard worked at that time for a French research organisation and, although an industrious worker, he was poorly paid. This did not deter him from giving up his job for an even less lucrative one when his company agreed to work for their new German masters. Hollard secured a position for another company which manufactured charcoal-burning gas generators for cars. As a representative of his new company, he was obliged to travel extensively throughout France, scouring the heavily-wooded areas for trees suitable for use in the production of charcoal. In the course of his travels he picked up information which he thought might be useful to the Allies. He resolved to get this to them and did so by crossing the frontier into Switzerland and establishing contact with a British agent there. But on his first attempt, he was captured by German troops manning the heavily-guarded frontier. It was his job that got him out of trouble. He pointed out that he was in that area searching for suitable supplies of wood for his company. Fortunately the Germans accepted his story and he was set free. His second attempt at getting over the border was successful and he made contact with a British agent who asked him to gather as much information as he could about such things as military strong points, the disposition of troops and their movements. Hollard agreed and returned to France.

During the course of the next three years he established himself as one of the Allies' most valuable spies, slipping across the frontier to pass on whatever important information he could gather. He faced the most incredible dangers in doing so and moments of high tension were regular and unwelcome events. The German Secret Service was hot on his heels but this did not deter him from carrying on his work, despite the threat to his wife and family whom he so dearly loved but so rarely saw.

Hollard was a 'loner', preferring to work on his own, but he found it necessary to recruit the help of many of his fellow countrymen to improve and widen the scope of his intelligence. His train of fellow agents grew until he found himself with some 120 workers, all ferreting out information under his direction. It was one of these who set Hollard on the trail of his most important discovery of the war.

In August 1943, the month during which the raids on Peenemünde and Watten took place, one of Hollard's agents was relaxing in a small cafe in the city of Rouen. While he refreshed himself with a drink the agent overheard two French building contractors discussing construction work that the Germans were engaged in near the coast. The agent, who had already been warned to keep an ear open for just this sort of thing lost no time in passing on the gist of this conversation to Hollard. It appeared that the contractors had mentioned that very large amounts of concrete were required for these constructions. And Hollard was quick to see that this might just be the secret construction work he had been told to look out for. Twenty-four hours later he was in Rouen, following up his agent's lead. But he was no longer the representative of a charcoal company. He wore a dark suit and posed as the representative of a religious organisation which cared for the spiritual needs of the workers. He visited the local employment office where he enquired if they knew of any large building sites nearby where he could begin his work. He proffered suitably inscribed bibles which convinced the official he spoke to of his occupation. The official thought for a moment, then referred to some records. Yes, there was such a site at a place called Auffey, about twenty miles from Rouen. Hollard thanked him profusely and left.

Hollard lost no time in getting to Auffey where, after some searching, he found the site. The area was a veritable hive of activity, swarming with countless workers, but the object of the work was not obvious from his vantage point. He realised that he would have to get inside and have a closer look. He divested himself of 'the cloth' and donned workman's clothes which he managed to procure. Returning to the site, he found a deserted wheelbarrow outside the perimeter of the work area and borrowed it, then wheeled it past the guard at the main entrance to the site.

Once inside, Hollard ditched the barrow and began a reconnaissance, carefully giving the impression that he was going about his lawful business and avoiding anyone who remotely resembled a foreman or overseer. After a look-see he engaged a worker in conversation and by devious dialogue learned that they were constructing garages.

'Strange place to build garages,' Hollard thought, 'and very robust buildings too. They don't look like garages and anyway, why would the Germans want garages twenty miles from the nearest town?'

Hollard was puzzled as he continued to make his way around the site. Then he came upon a long concrete ramp with a metal guideline running right up the centre. He was still puzzled until he realised in which direction the ramp was pointing. He pulled a compass from his pocket and surreptitiously took a bearing. The ramp pointed directly at the south-east of England. This was all he needed. Hollard casually left the site then made his way as quickly as possible to a contact who relayed his find to London. The reaction was immediate. London as always wanted more information. Were there any more sites and if so, where were they?

Hollard recruited the help of three more agents and they began a systematic search of northern France on bicycles. While they and other agents from different Underground groups scoured from the ground, RAF reconnaissance aircraft searched from the air. One after another more sites were discovered. In less than three weeks more than a hundred were uncovered in various stages of construction. The situation was fast reaching alarming proportions and the true extent of the onslaught that lay in store became terrifyingly clear.

By now, Hollard had become intent on laying his hands upon the exact plans of a launching site. By a stroke of good fortune, he learned that one of his agents had a friend by the name of André who had been engaged by the enemy to work on one of the sites at Bois Carré. Hollard persuaded the young Frenchman to draw a sketch of the site he was working on. At great personal risk, André did so, but the result was not detailed enough for Hollard who by now had his sights set upon a tracing of the master plan itself.

At first André was reluctant. He knew that the only copy of the master plan on the site was kept by the German in charge—and this was kept in his work coat pocket at all times. André puzzled over how he could get at the master plan. He watched the German like a vulture, waiting to pounce. Like most Germans, this one had regular habits and his morning visit to the toilet was no exception. Like clockwork, he went with almost ritualistic regularity—and this was the one and only time that he ever took off his coat and left it unattended with the master plan in the pocket. The German's ablutions were carefully timed by André. He took between three and five minutes every day.

One morning the German doffed his coat and went to the toilet. He was back five minutes later—but by then André had traced the master plan and returned it to the coat pocket. Thus armed, André dosed himself with a potion which Hollard had prepared for him. It brought on stomach pains. He was examined by a German doctor who could trace no illness but André convinced the sceptical physician by vomiting violently. The young Frenchman asked to be allowed to visit Paris to see his family doctor who had treated the complaint in the past. Permission was granted and André left for Paris—with the plans.

Hollard was staggered at the clarity of André's tracing. Combined with others he had 'acquired' from similar sources, he pieced them together to produce an amazingly accurate blueprint of a V-1 launching site. Now he was posed with the problem of getting this precious document to the British. Besides confirming that the first attack weapon would be by flying bomb and not rocket as some thought, the blueprint would enable the Allies to determine the best way of destroying the installations. Getting the plan to the British was of the utmost importance. Because of this, Hollard decided to deliver it himself via the tried and tested route across the Swiss frontier. By this time, October 1943, Hollard had crossed the frontier no fewer than forty occasions but the prize he now carried made this attempt by far the most important. As luck would have it, it was to prove the most hazardous and dangerous of his journeys.

On this occasion he chose the garb of a woodcutter, and as he slipped through the dense woods close by the frontier itself he was conscious of the close proximity of German patrols. The snap of a twig, the pant of a guard dog, a far-off bark, a guttural shout were the signals Hollard feared. Hidden in a sack of potatoes slung over his shoulder were the drawings. If he were caught with these, there would be no talking his way out of this one. Soon the barbed wire entanglement that represented the border came into view through the trees. Hollard was only yards away from his goal. A few more paces and he was by the thonged wire. His pulse raced as he threw the sack of potatoes over the fence and into Switzerland. Now it was his turn. He moved to jump over but there was a rustle behind him. He cast a glance round just in time to see the guard dog lunge at his leg. Its teeth sank into his flesh. He was caught fast. From the trees on the French side of the border came shouts. German voices yelled to the dog which had caught Hollard's scent and now held him captive.

Hollard writhed in agony. The dog's teeth had punctured the spy's knee and found the bone. Hollard could hear the Germans thrashing through the brush in the trees. They would have him soon. He had to get the dog's teeth free. He pulled at the animal's jaws to loose them but they were like a vice. Then he groped for a small broken branch which lay nearby. He grabbed it and rammed it between the locked jaws then twisted and thrust it down the dog's throat. For a few moments the animal held tenaciously on—it had been well trained. Then it sagged. Its teeth lost their grip and it fell dead to the ground. Hollard threw himself over the wire just as the German soldiers emerged from the trees. Their shouts to halt echoed in the trees. They levelled their rifles to fire. But no shot came. Only yards away from where Hollard lay was a Swiss frontier guard. He too had his rifle aimed—but not at Hollard. He was challenging the Germans. They had lost their man—and in a few days, the British had their plans.

(Michel Hollard later returned to France and continued his work, but he was eventually arrested by the Gestapo who subjected him to terrible torture. In spite of this he revealed nothing to them and they could prove nothing against him. He was sent to a concentration camp where he spent the remainder of the war. He survived and among the decorations he received was his admission to the British Distinguished Service Order. General Sir Brian Horrocks dubbed Hollard 'the man who saved London'.)

Hollard's discoveries, coupled with aerial reconnaissance, told the British where the blitz would come from and they assumed that the missiles that would be launched from these sites would be in the form of pilotless, remotely-controlled aircraft. But knowing from whence they would come was one thing; knowing precisely what they were was quite another. Again photographic evidence was wanted. They were to get it quite by chance . . .

At dawn on the morning of 28 November, 1943, Squadron Leader John Merrifield's Mosquito launched into the air from the runway at RAF Leuchars, about 15 miles south of Dundee, in Scotland. Merrifield and his navigator, Flying Officer Whalley, set course across the North Sea in a bid to carry out a photo-reconnaissance of Berlin. Efforts over the past few weeks to photograph the German capital had been thwarted by bad weather and on this day Merrifield hoped for better luck. But when the Mosquito neared its target he saw his luck was out. A thick blanket of cloud hid Berlin from view. But, never one to waste an opportunity, the Squadron Leader sought out other targets. The weather over the Baltic was good so he headed for there. Before leaving Leuchars he had been briefed on alternative targets to photograph if Berlin was again 'camera shy' that day so he set out to do so. The cameras housed in the Mosquito clicked and whirred as the aircraft overflew enemy airfields and shipping locations at Stettin and Swinemünde. Then Merrifield turned his attentions to the island of Usedom. At a point known as Zinnowitz there was supposed to be a new German radar installation. Merrifield duly covered the area but even with that done, there were still a few frames of film left in his cameras. He looked around for some worthy target and found it—the airfield at Peenemünde, still operational despite the hammering the area had received from his Bomber Command comrades in August. The Mosquito bolted across the airfield then, with all the film spent, headed for home. He was not to know it then but Merrifield's insistence upon never leaving a single frame of film unused, was to produce one of the most remarkable and revealing photographs of the war.

When the photographs of that mission finally reached

Babington-Smith at RAF Medmenham on 1 December, she combed them with her usual thoroughness for signs of the 'pilotless aircraft' launching ramps she had been briefed to look for. She went through them with meticulous care, scouring them through the stereoscope until finally she held her breath. Her eyes focused upon one tiny 'mark' on a print. She examined it closer. The shadow it cast revealed it was a ramp built up on earth. It was angled out to sea and at its base was 'a tiny cruciform shape'. Constance Babington-Smith and John Merrifield had 'found' Hitler's *Vergeltungswaffe* 1—the V-1 flying bomb.

The ramp, its shape, size and the fact that it was pointing out to sea, compared with those discovered in the north of France, proved beyond doubt that the planned blitz would be by flying bomb. It was Hitler's intention to fire some 50,000 of these bombs at England and London in particular at the rate of 5,000 a month beginning that December—the very month that the momentous discovery was made. It was not to be. Before a single flying bomb could be fired at England, the Allied air forces pounded all but a few of the launching sites to destruction. The second blitz of Britain was delayed by some six months and the first flying bombs did not fall until June, 1944. But the first attack aimed at London went off like a damp squib. Instead of the threatened waves of bombs, only ten were actually fired on 12 June and of these, only one reached the capital.

But the Germans had made a remarkable recovery and after a lull of three days, bombs were fired at a rate of between 100 and 200 a day. Many failed to reach their targets but those that did caused terrible casualties. To counter the onslaught, more and more anti-aircraft guns were placed in the south of England, together with a great string of barrage balloons. Between them, they exacted a small toll of bombs as they winged their way towards London and other targets. But the most effective deterrent was the RAF pilot in the new Tempest fighter.

When the RAF first challenged the flying bombs the pilots raked them with cannon fire and they exploded but the effect of the explosion often caused damage to the fighter. But a daring and novel way of defeating the bombs was devised. This required the fighter pilot to fly alongside the bomb with his wing tip just below that of the bomb then, with a flick of the wing, he knocked the bomb off course, making it unstable and causing it to plunge to the ground.

By the beginning of September, 8,600 bombs had been fired at England. Some never reached England, a few because of faulty guidance systems, others because of anti-aircraft fire but in the main they were stopped by fighters of the RAF which, before the bombardment by flying bomb ended in March 1945, had accounted for 1,300 of them. A total of 10,000 bombs were launched and 7,500 of them reached England. Of these 2,500 got through to their targets, killing 6,184 people and injuring 18,000 more.

The creeping advance of the Allies following the Normandy Invasion mopped up the sites. Had it not been for the courageous efforts of a host of agents, the RAF's photo-reconnaissance aircraft and the PIU, combined with Bomber Command, the invasion of Europe might not have taken place. The V-1 had been discovered, challenged and very largely nullified. Some of the *dramatis personae* of the V-1 saga played an equally important role in revealing the other menace that lurked in the shadows of the Reich's experimental stations—the V-2 rocket.

Following the devastating RAF raid on Peenemünde on the night of 17/18 August, 1943, the development of the V-2 rocket was switched to another secret experimental establishment. The RAF's bombs, although hampering the development of the rocket, did not stop it. Plans and rockets were extracted from the rubble and moved elsewhere. But the question was, where?

Little was known of exactly what the other weapon was. Reports received from agents in Luxembourg in 1942 and 1943 indicated the existence of a rocket but their information was sketchy and failed to convince all of the senior scientists and the British Intelligence Service. Again there were suspicions of a German 'plant'. The Luxembourg agents had acquired their information with what seemed comparative ease and this gave rise to doubts as to its veracity. But there were those in Britain who believed the reports, notably Professor R. V. Jones, a leading scientist. His most ardent opponent, Lord Cherwell, one of Churchill's closest advisers, firmly discounted the possibility that there might be anything bigger than the flying bomb. He believed that the pilotless flying bomb would be the German's only *Vergeltungswaffe*. When the raids began in June 1943, it was flying bombs and not rockets that came over. His prediction had, it seemed, been proved right. But Jones insisted there was an even greater threat, in the shape of a rocket which had the capability of travelling at over 3,000 miles an hour and could cause infinitely greater damage than the flying bomb. Cherwell scoffed—but Jones was right. He, unlike many of his colleagues, was one of the few who at the outset of the war had believed most of the revelations in the Oslo Report. Other snippets of information which had percolated through the espionage system had added weight to his belief, though they had been discounted by his colleagues.

At this stage even Churchill was inclined to the opinion that the rocket was a German hoax. The evidence—even that in the photo-reconnaissance photographs taken of the V-2s at Peenemünde—would have been part of an elaborate deception plan. The Germans were quite capable of inventing just such a scheme to fool the British. But Jones' firm belief that there was a much greater threat to come would not be shaken. Absolute confirmation of the Professor's theory was to come from two countries—Sweden and Poland.

Quite by chance, a V-2 rocket fired from somewhere in Poland—although its launching point could not be confirmed at the time—landed in Sweden and blew up, leaving fragments scattered over a wide area. These scraps were gathered up and handed over to the neutral Swedish government. There followed a race between the British and Germans to gain possession of these vital parts. The British won, by trading them for a consignment of tanks. But there were even greater things to come from the heart of Poland where the Polish Home Army, the equivalent of the Resistance movement in other countries, had perhaps the best organised espionage and intelligence system within any German occupied territory.

The intelligence section of the Home Army came under the command of Colonel Iranek-Osmecki, who had been parachuted into Poland in order to piece together an Intelligence Bureau shattered by sweeping arrests and summary executions. He was faced with an onerous task but in a remarkably short time he built up a first class network of agents. Like all other agents, they were trained to be on constant look out for anything that might prove of importance and the wealth of information that came out of Poland was very considerable, much to Osmecki's credit. But the biggest scoop was about to come when, during the months of November and December 1943, his agents began reporting furtive German activity in and around Blizna which lay in a deeply wooded area of western Poland. These reports indicated that trains had been seen carrying cargoes of what looked like aircraft fuselages. The old branch line leading to Blizna had recently been repaired and the sub-standard roads in the area resurfaced. Furthermore, and this gave even greater cause for concern and interest, several villages in that sector had been evacuated. Blizna, it was already known, had been, and in all probability still was, an SS artillery training establishment.

Osmecki's agents penetrated the wooded areas and lay in wait for the trains which passed that way *en route* to the camp. They photographed the canvas-covered loads then made their way nearer to the base itself. This was not the first time they had seen it but now they were in for a surprise. It had been greatly enlarged. There were more buildings and some new constructions and earthworks. It was later learned that the camp was now on the top secret list and indeed was so secret that not even German aircraft were allowed to overfly it.

The deeply wooded area in which the camp lay was heavily patrolled but the agents made their escape and all their information was sent off to Intelligence headquarters in Warsaw. It was clear that they had uncovered something big and Warsaw eagerly awaited more information.

It was about then that an event occurred which helped point towards the belief that Blizna was a rocket site. There was a car accident in Warsaw. Agents working in the hospital learned that the victims, three German civilians, were top scientists. They appeared to have been *en route* for the Blizna area.

News began flooding the Polish Home Army headquarters from then on. Twice, projectiles landed and exploded, leaving gaping holes in the ground. To Osmecki (code named Makari)* the evidence pointed irrefutably to some kind of 'aerial torpedo'.

Makary immediately set up a special unit to concentrate on gaining as much information as possible on the new weapon, this being their sole task. From London, the Polish General Staff and British Intelligence were screaming for more information on these

---

* Because of the complicated pronunciation of some of the Polish names, to ease the burden on the reader only code names will be used in the text from here on.

new discoveries. It was not long in coming.

In December, a whole series of sightings and violent explosions was reported, along with unusual German patrol activities in selected areas. It was in these areas that the projectiles invariably landed. Loyal peasants were enlisted to retrieve fragments of the rockets and there ensued a race between them and the Germans to see who could get to the rocket's landing point first. Invariably the peasants won and a mountain of these bits and pieces were hidden away then smuggled to Polish scientific experts in Warsaw where they were examined in detail. After each explosion, the German patrol arrived then picked up as many of the pieces of the wreckage as the peasants had left for them. There followed a systematic probe of the damage caused. The Germans measured the width and depth of the craters caused by the explosions. On more than one occasion, the rockets fell on villages wrecking houses and killing the inhabitants.

London wanted to know exactly what was going on at Blizna. To achieve this the redoutable Poles went to the extent of planning a raid on the SS camp but this was discounted as impracticable although, had London insisted, the Poles would undoubtedly have carried it out. But a stroke of luck was to make the raid unnecessary. . . .

On May 20, 1944, farmer Jan Lopaciuk was going about his business on his small farm when he heard the screech of a rocket and saw it plummet towards the ground not far from his farm. It landed in a swamp near the River Bug. But, although he had seen such things before and heard the resulting explosion, this time there was no resounding bang to shake the countryside. It had failed to explode. He raced to investigate and found the rocket jutting out of the swamp. It was, as far as he could see, still intact. Lopaciuk bolted to the surgery of the local doctor to tell him of what had happened and in no time Makary's agents were on the scene, ramming the rocket deeper into the swamp. It was a race against time for they knew that at any moment the German patrol would be on the scene but they succeeded in hiding the rocket from view before the patrol car hurtled down a dusty track towards the area. They had made it just in time and they scattered to hide nearby and watch with a combination of amusement and bated breath as the Germans carried out a hopeless search for their precious rocket. They never did find it.

A few nights later, three teams of sturdy horses were brought to the edge of the swamp and stout ropes attached to them and to the huge rocket. After a herculean struggle, the rocket was wrested from the swamp and towed to a nearby barn where it was hidden. By then the Germans had given up their search for it. They remained mystified and their opponents could do nothing for the moment but gloat in glee at their find.

Two leading scientific experts of the Home Army, 'Raphael' (Jerzy Chmielewski) and 'Korona' (Antoni Kocian) arrived from headquarters and began dismantling the giant missile, photographing all its vitals and packaging those which could be of further use in their investigation. Meanwhile outside, a tough looking band of Home Army volunteers stood guard.

The task facing the two experts, who were specialists in aeronautical engineering and were concerned in keeping a watchful eye on secret German scientific developments, was an enormous one. The rocket contained more than 25,000 parts. Each of these was either photographed, packed away or noted in a dossier which was growing into a massive tome.

Before their investigations were complete the first scraps of information were being radioed to London. When the news of the captured rocket reached the Polish General Staff and thereafter the British Chiefs of Staff, the prospect of a devastating raid upon Blizna was considered—but it had to be discounted because the bombers available at the time did not have the range (with a sufficiently large bomb-load) to reach Blizna. Even the newly captured airfields in north Italy, and that of Brindisi, were not close enough.

This did not however prevent Constance Babington-Smith's reconnaissance aircraft from carrying out sorties and confirming that the site was indeed that of a rocket launching area. But even the photographs of the site and the tit-bits of information smuggled out of Poland were not enough to convince men like Cherwell. If the full extent of the new threat were to be known definitely then he and men like him wanted to see the rocket itself or have some of its parts as positive proof.

With their investigations complete, Korona and Raphael pondered upon whether or not it would be possible to devise a system whereby they could interrupt the rocket's guidance system and send it off course. Such a method was in fact feasible but it would, they appreciated, take time to build up such a complex piece of equipment—and time was against them. By that stage in the war, the Russians were advancing rapidly from the east and the Germans prudently thought it advisable to move their experimental site to a safer place. The guidance interrupter system was no longer needed. But now London was hell bent on getting the vital rocket parts out of Poland along with the photographs and the mass of notes Raphael and Korona* had assembled.

A flurry of transmissions between London and the Home Army arranged that a Dakota aircraft would land at an old disused and deserted emergency airfield and pick up the rocket parts together with the photographs and documents. Raphael was to be entrusted with their safe delivery. The Dakota would land on the airfield and pick up Raphael and an entourage of other Poles and ferry them to Brindisi and thereafter to London with the vital possessions.

'Operation Wildhorn 111', the flight to pick up Raphael and his confederates, surprisingly did not take place until 25 July. By then, Raphael, the precious bundles of parts and all the other paraphernalia, along with his companions had been in position near the airfield while the German army was beginning its retreat from that area.

The airfield—in fact it was no more than a wasted meadow—lay about 45 miles east of Cracow and the agents waited in tense expectation for the night of the operation to arrive. The day preceding the night of the operation arrived and with it came torrential rain, which transformed the meadow into a soggy mess. This would make the landing and take-off of the Dakota difficult. But if that were not enough there were other problems in store. During that day, two German light aircraft landed in the meadow and German troops moved into the area. It seemed then that the flight might have to be cancelled. Mercifully, the two enemy aeroplanes took off later in the day—but the troops remained only a kilometer or so away. It was going to be a dodgy operation. The prospect of jeopardising the whole operation occurred to Raphael and he considered contacting Brindisi and

---

* On June 1, 1944, the Gestapo tracked down Korona and arrested him and his wife. Although his wife survived the war, Antoni Kocian was murdered, along with 104 others in the shambles of the Warsaw ghetto.

calling it off—but by then it was too late; the Dakota was already on its way.

Night came and with it, masses of local villagers to crowd the meadow. They had heard of the impending operation and were bent upon giving the Dakota a good welcome and helping in whatever way they could. Raphael could well have done without them but as events were to prove, it was fortunate that they did come.

The Dakota's flight from Brindisi was uneventful and finally it droned overhead, much to the joy of the Polish onlookers. But they all realised that by now the Germans would know of its presence. If they did not know then they certainly did when the Dakota's powerful landing lights shone to show the pilot the strip of sodden ground. He circled the meadow twice before making a landing. The wheels gouged deep furrows in the ground as the passenger aircraft touched down and came to a halt. The door was immediately thrown open and the incoming passengers leapt from the aircraft and disappeared into the night.

Willing helpers aided the boarding passengers and their parcels of parts onboard and the door was slammed shut. In the cockpit, the pilot started up the engines and released the brakes—but nothing happened. The Dakota had sunk into the muddy ground. The monster would not budge. She was stuck fast.

The passengers and their luggage were off-loaded while another attempt was made, again without success. By now the Germans were on their way to investigate and the precious minutes were slipping by fast. A hurried conference was held during which it was decided to abandon the flight, burn the aircraft and try another time. Petrol was already being thrown over the aircraft and a light about to be put to it when one of the Poles protested, insisting that another attempt to take off must be made. He ordered trenches to be dug in front of the Dakota's wheels and local villagers set about this with a will. When these were complete, they were filled with straw and wooden planks.

Once more the passengers and their cargo were reloaded. The engines roared into life, brakes released and the Dakota slid forward. It gathered speed and at last lifted into the air. With that, the villagers and the members of the Home Army melted into the background before German troops arrived to investigate a short time afterwards.

Raphael reached Brindisi safely and travelled on to London where he passed over all his precious luggage. There was absolutely no doubt now about the veracity of all the bits of information that had been filtered out of the occupied countries. There *was* a V-2 rocket. It seems incredible, but even then Cherwell and the other doubters *still did not agree that* it posed a major threat. Even Duncan Sandys, who had done so much in the investigation of German secret weapons, was still not absolutely convinced, despite a full report of all the findings which was passed to the military and civilian leaders. On 7 September, 1944, Sandys made a statement to the press which began, 'Except possibly for a few last shots, the Battle for London is over'. A little after tea time the following day in the Chiswick area of London, Hitler's *Vergeltungswaffe* 2, a V-2 rocket, landed, killing two people and injuring another ten. Seconds later, another fell at Epping. These two rockets were the first of some *one thousand, one hundred and fifteen* V-2s which hit England. Five hundred of these hit London. As a result of these attacks, 2,588 people were killed and another 6,268 seriously wounded. Paris, by then in Allied hands, was hit too, but the worst attack of all was intended for Antwerp in Belgium at which 1,500 V-2s were aimed.

The bulk of these rockets were fired from sites at the Hook of Holland, Leiden and the Hague where, thanks to Constance Babington-Smith's scrutiny of photographs from the reconnaissance aircraft, they were spotted, about to be launched from a city park and a racecourse.

The advance of the Allied armies and bombing of the factories where the rockets were built brought the rocket attacks to an end on 27 March, 1945. Were it not for the valiant work done by Robin, Raphael, Korona, Hollard, Babington-Smith and countless others in exposing the terror weapons, the flying bomb and the V-2, there might not have been an Allied but an Axis invasion.

4

The Impostors

On 1 May, 1915, New Yorkers opened their morning newspapers to see an unusual advertisement. It took the form of a warning, and one that was to presage one of the most heinous crimes committed in the bitter war that raged on and below the tempestuous Atlantic seas. The advertisement read:

'NOTICE! Travellers intending to embark on the Atlantic voyage are reminded that a state of war exists between Germany and her allies and Great Britain and her allies; that the zone of war includes the waters adjacent to the British Isles; that, in accordance with formal notice given by the Imperial German Government, vessels flying the flag of Great Britain or any of her allies are liable to destruction in those waters and that travellers sailing in the war zone on ships of Great Britain or her allies do so at their own risk.'

The warning was placed close by a Cunard Shipping Line advertisement announcing that their passenger ship, *Lusitania*, would sail from New York that day. Despite the German warning, almost two thousand passengers and crew boarded the ship and the luxury liner sailed on schedule for England.

Only twenty-four hours before *Lusitania* put to sea, another vessel sailed—not from New York but from its base in Germany, over three thousand miles away over the Atlantic. She was the German submarine, U-20, under the command of Commander Walther Schwieger. These two craft were fated to meet in a one-sided clash which was to shock the world.

Lusitania forged her way across the Atlantic, her plush saloons thronged with passengers. But as she cut her course across wild seas, U-20 was creeping through the English Channel to take up station in a favourite hunting ground of German submarines off the south-west coast of Ireland. *Lusitania* was four days out of

New York when U-20 scored her first 'kill', sinking a British sailing ship. The following morning she accounted for a British steamer and, later, another merchant ship. Schwieger was in good form and, buoyant with his success, sought further fodder for his guns and torpedoes. But for the two days that followed, Schwieger sighted no more worthy targets. His oil supply was running low and, with only two more torpedoes left, he decided to head back towards his base at Wilhelmshaven. A thick sea fog was closing in, making submarine hunting difficult, so it was a reasonably content Schwieger who turned for home on the morning of 7 May.

Shortly after 1400 hours on that same day, while U-20 was *en route* for Germany and submerged to a depth of twenty metres, Schwieger detected the sound of a ship's propellers. The pronounced sound of them indicated that the ship was a big one, so Schwieger brought U-20 to periscope depth. Peering through the periscope, he caught sight of a big, armoured cruiser which had just swept right over the top of the submarine and was now 'showing its tail' and ploughing through the waves away from him at high speed. There was no chance of shooting at her. He would be wasting a torpedo if he tried a stern shot; it was much too difficult. And there was no hope of him catching her up and setting up an attack. Schwieger cursed his luck. The cruiser would have made a fine trophy to round off a handsome 'bag' for the patrol.

As the cruiser drew farther away from the submarine, Schwieger saw that the weather was clearing. The fog was slowly lifting to reveal a clear, blue sky. Because of the range of vision, Schwieger thought it safe to bring the U-boat to the surface and continue on course for home until he reached the approaches to the English Channel. He could recharge his tired batteries by running under engine power on the surface.

The U-boat throbbed as she slid ahead with her engines pulsating. In the conning tower, look-outs leant over its rim and swept the seas with powerful glasses. Not long had passed since the sighting of the cruiser when one of the look-outs spotted a movement on the horizon. Schwieger focused his glass on the spot. Sure enough, there was something there. It looked like masts; at first glance, possibly several ships. But it soon became clear that it was just one ship—and a giant at that. Schwieger immediately ordered the submarine down to periscope depth and watched the ship, a passenger liner, move through the waves. She was on a heading towards U-20 but sailing a zig-zag course, a procedure used by ships' captains to fox enemy submarines. She made a fine and tempting target, despite the zig-zagging tactics which might make her more difficult to hit.

The following is an extract from the log of U-20 recorded as the action that followed took place.*

'2.20 pm. Directly in front of us I sighted four funnels and masts of steamer at right angles to our course, coming from south-southwest and going towards Galley Head. It is recognised as a passenger steamer.

'2.25 pm. Have advanced eleven metres towards steamer in hope it will change course along the Irish coast.

2.35. Steamer turns, takes direction to Queenstown, and thereby makes it possible for us to approach it for a shot. We proceed at high speed in order to reach correct position.

'3.10. Torpedo shot at distance of 700 metres going 3 metres below the surface. Hits steering centre behind bridge. Unusually great detonation with large cloud of smoke and debris shot above the funnels. In addition to torpedo a second explosion must have taken place. (Boiler, coal or powder?) Bridge and part of the ship where the torpedo hit are torn apart, and fire follows.

'The ship stops and very quickly leans over to starboard, at the same time sinking at the bow. It looks as though it will capsize in a short time. There is great confusion on board. Boats are cleared and many of them lowered into the water. Many boats, fully loaded, drop down into the water bow or stern first and capsize. The boats on the port side cannot be seen clearly because of the slanting position. At the front of the ship the name *Lusitania* in gold letters can be seen. The chimneys are painted black. The stern flag is not hoisted. The ship was going about twenty-three miles an hour.'

On board *Lusitania*, men, women and children fought to seek succour in the lifeboats. There were just not enough of them. Those that there were tipped and spilled their human cargoes into the sea that swelled hungry and menacingly, waiting to swallow them. Pathetic souls fought for their lives on the tilting deck,

---

* *Raiders of the Deep*, by Lowell Thomas. (Heinemann.)

grasping anything that might arrest their slide into the ocean. Frantic mothers and fathers battled through panic-stricken passengers to find their children. Husbands and wives were parted never to see each other again. Others fought and thrashed at those who scrambled for a place on a boat. Organised boat drill was hopeless.

Below decks passengers were trapped. As the great liner tilted over the plush decor cascaded down upon passengers and crew alike, trapping them beneath it. Great torrents of water poured through the labyrinth of corridors seeking out human prey, entombing men, women and children in saloons and cabins, there to die a slow death by drowning. The sea found its way through every crevice: open portholes, doors, hatches and the great gash ripped in the ship's side by the torpedo. *Lusitania* was doomed.

Schwieger was confident now that the ship would sink so there was no need to use his last torpedo. He left the area to return to Wilhelmshaven, leaving the liner to slip beneath the waves and the survivors to fend for themselves.

One thousand, one hundred and ninety-eight men, women and children lost their lives in that action and among these were one hundred and twenty-eight American citizens. In Germany Schwieger was hailed as a hero. Throughout the rest of the world he was condemned as a ruthless murderer of innocents.

Until February of that year, the German Navy had conducted a 'restricted' submarine campaign. This meant that, before sinking a British or Allied merchant ship, the submarine had first to surface, bring the enemy vessel to a halt and determine what cargo she was carrying. If the cargo was contraband, likely to be vital to the war effort, then the submarine commander was entitled to sink the ship, but not before ensuring that the crew and passengers had taken to their boats. Then, and only then, was he lawfully permitted to sink the ship. But all that changed in February 1915 when, under mounting pressure from his war lords, the German Kaiser gave the 'green light' for an unrestricted submarine campaign. His submarine commanders would now be allowed to sink *any* ship. The proclamation declared that from 18 February onwards all merchant ships found in the war zone around Britain would be sunk without prior warning and '*without it always being possible to avoid danger to the crews and passengers*'. The effect was immediate and dramatic. By the end of April, little more than two months after the unrestricted campaign began, Britain had lost thirty-nine merchantmen totalling some 105,000 tons. It was a devastating blow—but there was worse to come. The sinking of the *Lusitania* was just one example.

The Germans claimed on the one hand that the *Lusitania* was a legitimate target since she was said to be carrying weapons, ammunition and gunpowder as well as a consignment of gold. But this claim was vehemently denied by the British and American authorities who insisted that she was carrying no such cargo and, furthermore, was neither armed or escorted. In America, the sinking of the *Lusitania* did much to convert the anti-war faction, swaying them in favour of entering the war on the side of the Allies.

The fate of the *Lusitania* was a single incident in a fierce war of attrition waged by German submarines against Britain's Atlantic lifeline. In the course of the First World War, U-boats accounted for some nineteen million tons of shipping, over half of it British. This represented between five and six thousand ships. The submarine menace was, perhaps more than anything else, the greatest threat to Britain's survival of the war. The umbilical cord through which her war supplies came across the Atlantic was almost severed. So great was the menace that in April 1917, Admiral Jellicoe, the First Sea Lord, estimated that Britain had supplies of food and raw materials to last for only a further six weeks. 1917 was the worst year of all, with Britain losing over 2,000 ships to the U-boats. In the first six months of that year, over three thousand merchant seamen were killed at sea. The situation became so serious that some merchant seamen simply refused to sail until measures were introduced that would turn the tables on the Germans. Since some of these men had been torpedoed three or more times, it is hardly surprising that some of them opted not to sail again. It was in fact not until the introduction of the convoy system, when merchant ships sailed in groups under warship protection, that the U-boats found themselves on the losing side and the flow of food and war materials between Britain and the United States was restored.

Throughout the war, countless means were used to combat the U-boats in their bid to strangle Britain into defeat. They were hunted by myriad vessels, ranging from destroyers to trawlers and anti-submarine patrol vessels. None of them was outstandingly successful in combating the enemy submarine. In the whole war, only 178 German submarines were sunk, and not all of these as a result of action by Allied warships. Some struck mines, while others simply vanished without trace, a not uncommon event.

Methods devised to counter the submarine were many, some sensible, others ridiculous. Depth charges were introduced. These were bombs which were dropped from a surface ship to explode at a pre-determined depth. They were perhaps the most potent weapon employed against the submarine. But there were among the many inventions that flooded the Submarine Attack Committee at the Admiralty some that bordered on the lunatic. Legend has it that one wit suggested seagulls ought to be trained to sit on the periscopes of enemy submarines to make the U-boat more easily seen—a novel, if somewhat ridiculous precursor of the underwater sonar detection device. But if that one sounds crazy, there was another which capped even that for sheer incredibility. The suggestion was that expert swimmers should be recruited and form special anti-submarine units. Their function would be to swim out to a U-boat and puncture its steel hull with a hammer and chisel. It need hardly be said that neither of these suggestions was actually adopted as a method of countering the threat of the U-boat. But the well-meaning, if crackpot, inventors did not stop there. Another 'gem' was suggested. It was for the formation of another patrol which was to operate off Portland, the naval base on the Channel coat. This was to comprise a number of picket boats and on board these seamen who, upon sighting a U-boat, were to race to its position and attack the periscope with a hammer and smash the glass then tie a specially provided bag over the periscope to 'blind' its commander. The U-boat captain would, it was suggested, surface to discover what on earth was going on then be blown out of the water by gunfire from the picket boats. It apparently did not occur to the deviser of this system that, because the periscope was above the surface, the U-boat captain would be able to see the picket boat approaching in the first place and dive out of the way. Even if one periscope were wrecked, the U-boat had another it could use. Schemes like these were totally unrealistic and merely served to prove that the inventors at this time had a complete lack of knowledge of the submarine and its working.

Submarine warfare was new. Neither the British or, for that matter, the Germans, had any experience of it and therefore all the anti-submarine devices and tactics had to be original inventions. Learning the lessons of combating the submarine was costly, both in terms of lives and ships lost. But not all the suggestions that found their way to the Submarine Attack Committee, whose job it was to assess and develop methods of fighting the submarine, were useless. There were those, such as the depth charge and the underwater detection device, that were to play a large part in revolutionising the struggle against the submarine. One method of attack was to be put into action quite early in the war and provide some of the most heroic and hair-raising incidents of the entire war at sea. This was the Q-ships, apparently innocent-looking merchant ships, manned by Royal Navy crews, that hid a powerful sting and lured U-boats to their doom.

U-boat commanders developed a technique for dealing with unarmed merchantmen. Torpedoes were extremely expensive weapons and therefore were conserved for use against armed ships. Since the lone, unarmed merchant ship sailing without an escort could put up no fight and since the U-boat commander had, according to the rules laid down, to first establish the cargo she was carrying before sinking her, he could surface without fear of retaliatory attack, bring the merchant ship to a halt with a shell across her bows, then examine her cargo and papers before sinking her by gun-fire. This enabled him to keep his torpedoes for use against warships if and when the opportunity arose. Such tactics were frustrating for the merchant crews. There was little they could do to stop such 'piracy'. But there was a chink in the U-boat's armour. While on the surface and with all her hatches open, she could not dive quickly out of harm's way. The deck crew manning the gun and the commander in the conning tower had to get below decks and secure the hatches before the submarine could dive.

It was this moment of vulnerability that set the experts thinking. Their deliberations brought about the innovation of the Q-ship. The element of secrecy was of the utmost importance and the disguise would have to be perfected and pass the closest scrutiny by the U-boat commander at sea. It was realised that if the Germans were in any way suspicious of the apparently innocent merchantman then he would simply sink her by torpedo. It was vital, if the Q-ship action were to be a success, that the U-boat was lured to the surface. The Q-ship's hidden guns could then be brought to bear and hopefully puncture the submarine's casing.

The art of camouflage both for the ship itself and the crew who would have to appear like any other merchant crew had to be mastered but, although certain guidelines were laid down by the Admiralty, the execution of the Q-ship's action was largely left to the individual commander.

Sailing in a Q-ship was to be a singularly dangerous pursuit. The ship would ply the regularly used sea lanes and blatantly lay itself wide open to attack—indeed, invite attack. When a U-boat had fired at the ship and possibly inflicted some damage, a 'panic party' would simulate the 'abandon ship' and take to the boats, then pull away from the 'stricken' vessel. Behind them they would leave another full crew who, out of view of the submarine, would wait until the U-boat got into range, when the disguise would be shed and with luck and a good aim, the guns would sink her. That, in essence, was the system the Q-ships would adopt. As we shall see, it was sometimes to go fatally wrong.

The greatest exponent of the art of Q-ship warfare was Gordon Campbell. As a young lieutenant in command of the destroyer *Bittern* in September 1915, he suddenly found himself unemployed when, in his anxiety to track down and attack a 'submarine', one of the engines was wrecked beyond repair and the destroyer had to limp back into Plymouth. Campbell's 'submarine' had been nothing more suspicious than a new seaplane carrier out on trials. His race had been in vain and his ship put out of commission. Now he found himself without a ship and still itching for a scrap with the enemy. He was not to know it then, but his encounters with the enemy were not to come in sleek, fast destroyers or indeed anything remotely resembling the warships he had been used to.

Campbell had heard whispers of 'mystery ships' which were engaged in an unconventional form of warfare against the U-boats. The Admiralty had gone to great lengths to keep the activities of its Q-ships a secret, even among Royal Navy personnel—and in later years this was to cause Campbell some embarrassing, amusing and sometimes annoying moments.

Campbell was a man of action, moulded in the true tradition of the Royal Navy. He was at home only when he was at sea and detested inactivity, especially when there was a war on. As a professional sailor, he felt that in wartime he should be in the thick of the fighting. His *modus operandi* was about to change, but in the meantime Campbell had to cool his heels on dry land. It was a frustrating interlude for him, especially when his comrades returned from sea with tales of adventure. Then one day he got a call to go to the Admiralty. Throughout the train journey to London he speculated upon what might be in store for him; possibly a new command or an appointment to a cruiser or battleship. Anything would be preferable to inactivity. But when he arrived at the Admiralty he found a surprise in store for him. Campbell was 'asked' to volunteer for 'special service'. It was a polite form of order. But the prospect of engaging in something special intrigued the Lieutenant—although he was not told what sort of work he would be engaged in. However, a hint was dropped when he was asked if he had heard of the *Baralong*. Campbell knew the name and had heard rumours that she was engaged in some sort of anti-submarine work. His curiosity and excitement were roused and he 'volunteered' with alacrity. He would, he was told, serve under Admiral Sir Lewis Bayly. Although he had never met Bayly, Campbell knew him to be a 'no nonsense' Commander-in-Chief who was based at Queenstown, a port on the south coast of Ireland.

Promoted to Lieutenant Commander, Campbell was ordered to Devonport to await the arrival of his new command, a ship by the name of *Loderer*. The sight that met his eyes when she sailed into the harbour from Cardiff left her new captain speechless. The *Loderer* was a weather-worn old tramp, covered in grime and carrying a cargo of coal. Campbell's heart sank. This, he thought, must surely be the bottom of the barrel. For the seasoned naval officer, used to the spit and polish of one of His Majesty's ships of war, this seamy old tramp was the last straw. He felt that he had been given command of the ancient tub as a sort of punishment for some past misdeed, but he could think of nothing he had ever done that would warrant such treatment. Campbell saw what had been a promising career in the Royal Navy crumble before his eyes. This was the ultimate insult.

In truth, he had been paid a great compliment, for as he was later to discover it was only the cream of the navy who were to be given such commands.

The air of mystery that surrounded the operations in which he was to take part was so complete that, for the moment, Campbell thought that no-one was going to share the secret even with him. He received no written orders and nothing had been said to him before the ship docked. It was only when the *Loderer* was securely tied up at Devonport that the Dockyard Superintendent told him he had been allocated three twelve-pounder guns and a Maxim. Campbell wondered for a while what he was expected to do with them and was about to ask when at last he was told by word of mouth precisely what his new function was to be. He had unwittingly become one of His Majesty's Q-ship commanders. Now things began to make sense. The tramp was an obvious choice. What U-boat commander would suspect a tramp steamer of being a fighting ship? The more Campbell thought about it, the clearer it became to him that he had just the ship for the job. But now he had to face the task of fitting her out for her new role.

Almost at once, Campbell decided to run the ship as he would run a man-of-war—below decks, at least. Outwardly, she would be a merchant vessel, but behind her innocent exterior would lie a fighting ship with a crew trained to the highest standards found in the Navy's warships. It would be difficult since, from the outset, Campbell would have to undo some of the disciplines which had become deeply ingrained in the crew during their Navy careers. Outwardly they would have to act and behave like merchant seamen, whose sense of discipline was far removed from that of the Royal Navy. Their smart naval uniforms would also have to go, of course. It would give the game away to a U-boat commander if he saw a dirty old tramp steaming along with a smartly dressed naval-looking type striding along the deck. Every detail had to be thought of if the disguise was to be perfected. The first thing, however, was the business of fitting out the ship. It was with a sense of excitement that Campbell began to pore over the plans and mark out the alterations he would require to transform her into a fighting vessel. Since the whole object of the Q-ship was to attack by surprise, it was essential in reshaping the ship to position the weapons so that they could be made ready for firing on the enemy submarine in an instant. To achieve this, they would have to be situated on the deck, but this posed a problem. How were weapons the size of twelve-pounders to be planted on deck without being seen by a U-boat crew? This was where improvisation was to come into play. He dared not cover the weapons with anything that would seem out of place on the tramp. Any unusual 'bump' on the deck or superstructure might well give rise to suspicion and result in the ship being sunk without the submarine surfacing.

Campbell studied his new command carefully. She was a typical tramp, of 3,200 tons, 325 feet long and 45 feet in the beam. When he took her over she was loaded with over 5,000 tons of good Welsh coal but to his disgust he found that she was in fact greatly overloaded—a danger that he would have to rectify. The *Loderer* had a top speed of only 8 knots which, although not uncommon among tramps, might, Campbell thought, prove a disadvantage when he got into action. Only experience would tell.

Campbell was fortunate in having as his First Lieutenant a man with experience in the Merchant Marine; Lieutenant Beswick, RNR. He knew him of old, since Beswick had served under Campbell on his previous command, the *Bittern*. Beswick's knowledge of tramps was to prove invaluable, since he was able to advise Campbell upon what would and wouldn't 'do' on such a vessel. He was also to give his captain some useful tips on Merchant Marine procedure, ranging from the correct method of addressing officers, which was quite different from that used in the Royal Navy, to the sort of clothes that might be worn on a tramp steamer.

Between them, Campbell and Beswick selected the most suitable sites for the weapons. The first, a 12-pounder of some 18 hundredweights, was positioned at the stern of the ship and hidden within a specially constructed housing which looked exactly like a steering engine house. To add authenticity to its appearance, it was fitted out with a steam pipe which led from the real steam engine amidships along the deck and over the stern. It puffed out steam, which added to the impression that the housing contained an engine and not a gun. To be really effective, the housing which hid the gun had to be capable of collapsing when the call to action came. All four sides of the house were hinged and held in place by wires which could be 'slipped' when the command to open fire was given. The sides then fell away, giving the gun a clear area of fire.

The other two 12-pounders were placed amidships on either

side of the deck so that a broadside of two 12-pounders could be fired. To accommodate and hide the guns, the sides of the ship were cut and hinged. The hinges, which allowed the flaps to fall away enabling the guns to fire, were on the outside and visible, so they had to be camouflaged. Campbell was leaving nothing to chance. The hinges were covered with rubber to make them look like rubber strakes for going alongside a jetty. The gun ports, as the flaps were called, were held in place by simple bolts and pins which could be knocked out to expose the guns.

In addition to these weapons, a Maxim was mounted on the boat deck near the ship's single funnel. It was hidden from view by being placed in a hen coop which in turn was covered with tarpaulin. The hen coop was hinged half way down each side to allow the sides to drop.

Some time later, Campbell acquired another two 12-pounder and two 6-pounder guns. The two larger guns were housed in dummy cabins built on to the main deck. These too were equipped with hinges. The 6-pounders were located at either side of the bridge and the ends of the bridge hinged. These two smaller guns were a problem, though. They were the only guns which were visible to anyone on board the ship who cared to have a look round, so they had to be stowed away while the ship was in harbour, lest the *Loderer*'s true identity be given away. Such was the need for absolute secrecy that not even the pilots who navigated the ship into harbour were allowed into the secret.

The interior of the ship had to be virtually gutted to house the eleven officers and fifty-six men who made up the two crews. Accommodation was a major problem, since the ship had, in its days as a legitimate tramp carried a full complement of only thirty-two officers and men. It was essential that the men be kept hidden, so the accommodation had to be arranged in such a way that the crew could get to the guns without coming on deck. If a U-boat commander were to see milling about the deck more than the normal number of crewmen a tramp would carry, he might become suspicious and fire a torpedo. A warren of passageways therefore had to be built within the ship. Space for ammunition was another difficulty. The guns were to be kept loaded at all times and a supply of shells kept by each gun. Reserves of ammunition were kept in lockers on the mess deck. This was the only space available, although it was singularly dangerous, since a torpedo hit in that area would mean almost certain death for most of the crew.

Communication between Campbell and the crew when they were at action stations would be by voice pipe. He had toyed with the idea of a series of telephone links, but if the ship's electrical system were put out of action or simply failed to function, the result might be disastrous.

A number of other features were incorporated, some quite small, others large, but all essential to the ruse. Quick change acts would, Campbell realised, be vital to their operation. He ordered a whole supply of paints of various colours with which to paint and repaint the ship's funnel. This would be done at night so that she could change her identity. He also took on board a variety of flags to fly to complete the ruse. As we shall see this was to prove invaluable in the clandestine war on the German submarines. Among the other features dreamt up by Campbell were facilities for slotting new ship's names into specially prepared slots both on the bows and at the stern; easily movable lightweight deck cargoes; derricks which could be shifted to different parts of the ship and a telescopic mast which could be heightened or lowered, depending upon which type of tramp Campbell wanted his ship to be. But the *pièce de résistance* was the portable dummy donkey-boiler funnel, sited either just before or after the main funnel. The real donkey funnel was housed inside the dummy one so that it (the real one) could be exposed, and the larger dummy funnel could be placed either in front of the funnel or behind it. Campbell heard of an ingenious trick employed by another Q-ship commander who put a man inside the donkey funnel as a look-out.

Throughout all the modifications which were in progress, Campbell had to insist upon the strictest security surrounding the ship. Only a limited number of specially-chosen workmen were allowed on board. He knew that the slightest leak about what was going on on board would mark the *Loderer* as a Q-ship and if the information reached Germany, she would be doomed.

Refitting the ship into a disguised fighting unit was a formidable task which taxed Campbell's ingenuity, but equally difficult was the problem of selecting a crew to man the mystery ship. Contrary to popular belief, the men who made up the ship's complement were not volunteers, as one might suspect, this being a somewhat unconventional and extremely hazardous form of warfare. There were fifty-six of them, and each and every one had to match up to the high standards set by Campbell. While he had to maintain the basic, rather rigid discipline of the Royal Navy, Campbell had at the same time to convert his officers and men into merchant marine sailors, a difficult task since they were all imbued with instinctive discipline because of the rigorous training they had undergone in naval warships.

His crew was a motley bunch with very few regular career sailors. The vast majority of them had elected to join the Navy when war broke out. They came from every walk of life but Campbell was to mould them into the most effective and famous band of buccaneers of any Q-ship. With piratical intent, Campbell poached two of his officers from the Merchant Marine. One of them was Beswick, who had already served with him, but the other had never been on a man o' war. This man was to wreath himself in glory. Until he fell into Campbell's clutches he had been an Engine Room Artificer who had already served on the *Loderer* as Second Engineer Officer, the equivalent of a Chief Petty Officer in the Royal Navy. However, by devious means, Campbell engineered his demobilisation and had him commissioned as an Engineer Lieutenant RNR. Campbell was never to regret that appointment. The officer, Lieutenant Loveless, was to emerge as one of the most courageous of Campbell's crew. Another who was to distinguish himself was a very young officer, Sub-Lieutenant Nisbet.

As the other members of his crew made their appearance, Campbell's heart sank. They had been drawn from every corner of the Royal Navy and since the drafting officer was not privy to the secret of the Q-ship and had imagined that they were intended for service on an ordinary collier, he had not been over-zealous in picking the cream of the Navy. Campbell would in a very short time weed out the ones who were patently unsuitable for the dangerous task ahead, but these were very few. It was with considerable surprise that he found how adaptable and full of fight his officers and men were to prove. Among his new charges were men who, in civilian life, had been market gardeners, fishermen, merchant seamen, commercial travellers, factory workers and farm hands. It seemed as if the drafting officer had purposely chosen men with every conceivable kind of talent. Unwittingly, he had done Campbell an enormous service.

But Campbell made one horrific discovery after interviewing

his crew. Not a single man among them had ever steered a ship. One Irishman claimed that he had been a yachting enthusiast and could handle a tiller, but there was a vast difference between pottering about in a small sailing dinghy and steering a 3,000 ton collier laden with coal.

Campbell was understandably concerned about this and stomped off the ship to try to find a helmsman. It was in pursuit of the seemingly unattainable that he made his prize catch. He was about to enter the barracks where he hoped to find a suitable candidate, when he caught sight of a man whose weatherbeaten and heavily lined features gave him the stamp of a seasoned sailor. The old salt was wandering aimlessly outside the barracks, hands thrust deep into the pockets of his shabby trousers, and a pipe jutting from his mouth. Campbell went up to him, as if to engage him in casual conversation. The old sailor seemed totally disinterested, but halted his shambling walk, waiting for Campbell to speak but not bothering to turn to face him. The pipe belched a great cloud of smoke that almost screened him from Campbell's view. The Lieutenant Commander coughed as the cheap shag attacked his throat, but he succeeded in spluttering a 'Good morning'. There was no reply.

'I wonder . . .' Campbell began, now becoming annoyed at the old tar's reluctance to acknowledge him, 'I wonder, have you ever steered a ship?'

A sudden metamorphosis took place. The seaman grabbed the pipe from his mouth, turning on Campbell who was clad in civilian clothes and bore no mark of his rank. The older man's eyes narrowed. The spit which followed was projected several yards and indicated unmistakably that he had been insulted. His eyes gleamed at the impertinence of the question.

'Steered a bloody ship! I've steered the biggest bloody ship you've ever seen, mister. I's Quartermaster on the *Titanic* and I's Chief Quartermaster on the *Olympic* now. What d'you mean, steered a bloody ship? I could steer any damn tub that floats.'

Campbell muttered an apology, although he need not have done, for it was hardly warranted. He had no way of telling anything about the man, short of the obvious fact that he had been to sea. However, Campbell was no fool and realised that he had found his man. With some reluctance, the man informed Campbell that he was Jack Orr. Here was a gem not to be lost.

But it was clear that this old salt would have to be handled with kid gloves if Campbell was to succeed in recruiting him.

Campbell had to broach the subject with great tact, but, mustering all his skills of subtle persuasion, he managed to get Jack Orr to agree to join the ship's company. In his book*
Campbell reports that Jack Orr proved to be 'a brilliant helmsman and an excellent servant'. He was a handyman without peer whose many talents included hairdressing, tattooing and carpentry. He was to remain with Campbell until the end of the war.

Orr was absolutely loyal and dependable and proved himself heroic in the heat of battle, but Campbell recalls that he never once saw him laugh. Gritty, and apparently with no vestige of humour, he was nevertheless one of Campbell's most treasured assets on board ship.

Campbell earmarked those of the crew who would need careful watching. Any who gave signs, however small, of not matching up to his strict requirements were destined to go—and soon. Although outwardly his crew would follow the somewhat lax discipline of the Merchant Marine, Campbell was resolute in his determination that his discipline would really be rigid. In addition to the discipline imposed by Campbell, will-power of the highest order was essential, especially in times of great danger.

Once his crew was assembled, Campbell had to mould them into merchant seamen—wolves in sheep's clothing. They would wear civilian clothes at all times, both ashore and on board ship. Below decks, however, and while in action, they would retain the fighting spirit of naval seamen.

Following *Loderer*'s commissioning, appropriately on Trafalgar Day, 1915, Campbell set about kitting out his crew. He was, outwardly at least, no longer an officer of the Royal Navy, but Master of a tramp *Loderer*, and he himself had to look the part. He borrowed a tattered old cap from a merchant officer and wore it at a suitably rakish angle, while the rest of his apparel comprised a donkey jacket and a pair of trousers which would have been discarded as 'past it' by any self-respecting gardener. A glance in the mirror revealed nothing of the smart appearance of a clean-cut young naval officer. Now at least he looked the part. To

---

* *My Mystery Ships* (Hodder & Stoughton.)

complete the outward man he grew a handsome moustache, which was of course not permitted in the Royal Navy. But although he looked like a tramp's master, he had yet to become fully acquainted with the jargon and terminology of a Merchant ship's captain, which was quite different from a naval officer's. Orders were given in what to Campbell was a foreign tongue. His first Lieutenant, Beswick, became his 'Mate', the Engineer Officer his 'Chief' and so on. The men too had to be kitted out. Beswick and another of the officers, Truscott, were given the task of obtaining civilian clothes for the crew and they had to obtain them by somewhat devious means to avoid arousing suspicion. The Admiralty in its generosity allotted each officer three pounds and each man thirty shillings to kit himself out. It would have seemed odd if these two men had gone to a second-hand clothes dealer and asked for fifty-five assorted outfits, so they had to do the rounds of the rag stores and second-hand clothes dealers and buy a couple of suits and oddments at a time. It was a lengthy business but at last the entire crew was suitably dressed—and a dirtier, scruffier bunch of ruffians had never been seen on one of His Majesty's ships.

So effective was their disguise that even their friends found difficulty in recognising them, and they were treated with some disdain by their mates in the Royal Navy. Campbell, for example, was walking along the quayside one day when he caught sight of a cousin of his. Without thinking, he marched up to him and greeted him warmly. Campbell's cousin, immaculate in the uniform of a naval officer, was astounded by the sudden familiarity shown by this grubby old salt and asked who the devil he thought he was, accosting an officer of the Royal Navy. It took some persuading on Campbell's part to prove his identity. However embarrassing the incident was, it proved the effectiveness of the disguise, for if he could fool his own kin, then he would surely stand a good chance of fooling anyone who might spot him through the periscope of a U-boat.

Although Campbell's crew of 'ruffians' now merged into the merchant scene and could pass for merchant seamen in the dockyard cafés, there was still a great deal of work to be done on them. With the invaluable aid of the ex-merchant seamen among them, notably Loveless and Beswick, Campbell was able to shape routines for the 'merchant' operation of the ship. He knew how to deal with men below decks and there were in effect two sets of discipline: that which the U-boat commander would see in operation, and that suitable to the running of a fighting ship, which went on below decks. It was a powerfully difficult aim to achieve, but Campbell did it. His eagle eye spotted the slightest defect in the appearance of the men and the way they worked. Merchant seamen, unlike their naval counterparts, rarely 'doubled' when given an order. They performed their duties at their own pace. When cruising at sea, luring the U-boat, Campbell would have to ensure that there was an almost casual air among the deck crew. He had to instil into each man an automatic sense of transformation when they emerged from below decks. Scrubbing the deck of an old tramp was almost unheard of. Men had to be seen leaning over the rails, smoking a pipe or cigarette, careless of what might be lurking beneath the sea. An air of disinterest had to be apparent on deck. Washing would flutter on an improvised clothes line. In fact, almost everything that was strictly forbidden on the deck of a warship was positively on display on the *Loderer*'s deck.

To add another touch of reality to the scene, one of the ship's company was detailed to dress as a woman. In those days it was often customary for the master's wife to accompany him, and after some considerable persuasion one of the crew 'volunteered', much to the delight of ship mates and his own embarrassment.

To Campbell's surprise and delight, the crew entered into the spirit of the Q-ship with great enthusiasm, often adding their own touches to perfect the disguise. Campbell made it clear to them that the success of their operations depended upon every single individual on the ship. They each had a part to play—and they were to play it well. Their acting ability would have done credit to any Thespian.

Now that their guise was complete, they had to get down to the serious business of training but before doing so, Campbell went to great lengths to explain in minute detail what would be required of every man. He emphasised that they had to look and act like merchant seamen, even while in port. They all had to learn the terms used by merchant seamen even, and take care to use them, especially when the pilot was on board, for their secret was to be kept even from their own countrymen. The slightest flaw in the make-up would certainly expose them—and people were known to talk; as the posters of the time proclaimed to all, 'careless talk costs lives'.

The crew of the Q-ship was divided into two quite distinct categories. Although everyone on board was regarded as a combatant, for practical purposes they were divided into 'combatants'—those who were to man the guns and fight—and 'noncombatants', who were to make up the so-called 'panic party'. The gun crews had to reach the peak of efficiency in the operation of their weapons and of the torpedoes and depth charges when they were later installed. It was the gun crews who would remain on board after the 'panic party' had abandoned ship; they were the ones who would have to play the waiting game and endure the tense minutes or even hours after the boat had been shelled or torpedoed before discarding their mask and opening fire on the enemy submarine. Their gunnery had to be perfection. The accuracy of the first shots would be vital in any encounter, for a submarine could of course quickly crash dive out of harm's way. Campbell promised intensive gun drill—and kept his promise. The men who remained on board had to have nerves of steel, since in all probability the ship, having been shelled or torpedoed, would be sinking beneath them. It was made clear that if any one of them as much as moved into the sight of the U-boat commander, showing that the boat was not in fact abandoned once the 'panic party' had fled, there was a very good chance that the submarine would continue shelling her from a distance or put a torpedo into her. This was to become more and more important later when the existence of Q-ships became known to the German Navy. Courage of the highest order was therefore a prerequisite for manning the guns on a Q-ship.

The panic party, on the other hand, had an equally vital role to play in the game of duplicity. Their 'act' had to be flawless to convince the U-boat commander that they had left the ship deserted. Then, and only then, would a German submarine surface, having torpedoed the ship, and begin to finish her off with gunfire. On the other hand, if she had shelled and disabled the ship by firing at her from a distant range, outside that of the Q-ship's guns, she would only venture close to the stricken ship if her captain was secure in the knowledge that the ship was abandoned.

It was the custom of the German U-boat commanders to surface and close the lifeboats which contained the survivors of the 'sinking' merchantman to ascertain the name of the ship and the nature of her cargo. The reason for this was simple. The U-boat captain could claim a 'kill' only if he was able to positively identify the ship he had sunk. Few Germans would miss the opportunity of officially adding another British ship to their score. It was this factor that Campbell and other Q-ship captains banked upon to lure their prey within range of their guns.

Campbell proved himself a brilliant director of the theatricals essential to a convincing panic party. His intention was to create a scene of alarm and confusion, culminating in the abandonment of the ship. This he did with consummate skill.

At this early stage of the war there was no form of armament on board the average British merchantman so, if challenged by a U-boat, the crew had no alternative but to abandon ship. Fleeing the scene in a ship capable of a top speed of eight knots was out of the question, since the submarine could better that if she rode on the surface. In addition, without armament there was no means of fighting back so it was a one sided battle. When a legitimate tramp or more sophisticated merchant ship came under U-boat attack there was quite naturally a degree of panic and urgency about getting off the ship before she was sent to the bottom. A touch of sheer genius was evident when Campbell devised the drill for the panic party.

Through the periscope, the U-boat commander would see a handful of men engaged in workaday duties on the Q-ship's deck or simply lolling about. But far from being disinterested, these men were the eyes of the Q-ship, constantly alert and on the watch for the tell-tale metal finger protruding from the sea. When a periscope was sighted, Campbell emphasised, no hint of its discovery was to be visible. To all intents and purposes, the activity on the deck was to continue as it had been but news of the sighting would be quickly passed by word of mouth. It was then that the alarm would be raised below decks and the gun crews who were not already manning the guns would race to their action stations to await further orders from Campbell on the bridge. If the ship were torpedoed the reaction of the panic party would be immediate and the abandon ship procedure begin without delay. If she were shelled then a hit or a 'fake hit' would have to be scored before Campbell would give the order for the panic party to do their stuff.

The routine for abandoning ship, although ostensibly chaotic, would be carefully rehearsed. In the months that followed, these rehearsals were to become so routine that the panic party could carry them out without direction. But at the outset, Campbell drummed the procedure into his men until they lived the part. When the order to abandon ship was given, those men actually on deck would make a bee-line for the boats. Men would appear in a frenzy of panic, tumbling and falling out of the fo'c'sle, darting out from the stoke hold and engine rooms. Others would race about 'not knowing what to do'. Some would yell for help, for although these shouts would not be heard by those in the submarine, they would at least help the 'actors' to add a touch of realism to the scene.

In the panic to lower the boats, one of them would be allowed to fall 'with a run', in other words end up, spilling out the men inside it. Throughout the lowering of the boats and the boarding of them by the 'fugitive' it was essential that the apparent lack of practised drill should delay the men's departure from the ship. It was Campbell's theory that while this drawn-out charade was being enacted the U-boat would creep closer to the ship and therefore within range of the Q-ship's guns. While confusion reigned on the deck, the officer who was to play the part of the ship's master and take over from Campbell would swop hats with Campbell and make his way to the boats. Meanwhile, Campbell would duck down on the bridge and through small ports in the bridge observe the progress of the submarine. It was from this prone position that he would direct the operation against the submarine and eventually give the order to fire.

When the ship's company was safely on board the boats, complete with the ship's pet (stuffed) parrot, a further delaying tactic was employed. A grimey stoker would suddenly appear on the deck and yell for all he was worth to the boats pulling away from the ship, as if he had been forgotten and left behind. This meant that one of the boats would have to return to the ship and pick him up. It was hoped that by this time the submarine would be well within the range of the Q-ship's guns and running on the surface to intercept the boats and interrogate the ship's 'master'.

A star performance was required of all on board the boats, for by now they would be clearly visible to the captain of the submarine even through a periscope and even to the extent of their facial expressions which had to range from complete hopelessness to anger and fear. The panic party would continue to pull away from the stricken vessel, leaving it to await its fate. In fact by doing so they were acting as a lure and would steer a course to bring the submarine into the direct line of fire from the Q-ship, preferably where the Q-ship could get the maximum number of guns trained on her.

From his position on the bridge Campbell would keep a close watch on the submarine. It was entirely up to him to choose the moment to break out the White Ensign and shed the disguise, then open fire. That decision could make or break the entire attack. Not until the order to open fire was given did a single man dare to move on board the Q-ship. Campbell had to choose his moment: the moment when the submarine was well within range and with her captain on the bridge, the crew on deck and the hatches open. The first few shots were the ones that would decide the issue. Campbell realised only too clearly that if the submarine was not mortally wounded in the first salvo, she would escape and not only stand off and torpedo the Q-ship but return to base and expose the ship for what it really was. Then the secret would be out.

With his crew suitably indoctrinated, Campbell, a firm believer in on-the-spot practice at sea, took the *Loderer* out on short cruises where the crew was subjected to an intense round of practice in areas which Intelligence knew to be safe from the enemy. The practice included panic party abandonment of the ship and gunnery. To achieve proficient aim, a dummy conning tower was rigged and dropped into the sea then the guns would open up at it. As a consequence of these dummy runs and firing practice they acquired a very high degree of accuracy. But Campbell and the crew knew only too well that there was no substitute for the real thing and they itched to get on with the job.

It was towards the end of October 1915 that the announcement was made. *Loderer* had been sunk with all hands. She had been seen to leave port with a cargo of coal and the report was that she had been torpedoed and lost. The *Loderer* was 'gone'—but this was of course merely a craftily contrived piece of fiction. She was alive and well and sailing for her new base at Queenstown in the south of Ireland, but under the new name of HMS *Farnborough*, the 'true' name under which she was to operate. Now Campbell could adopt any disguise he wished. But since there was a remote possibility that the *Loderer*'s true identity might have leaked while she was being fitted out, Campbell thought it prudent to 'sink' her. The *nom de guerre* of the Q-ship *Farnborough* was to change many times in the months that followed.

The rusty old tramp finally put into Queenstown and it was there that Campbell first met the Commander-in-Chief, Admiral Bayly, with whom he was to strike up a lasting friendship and who was to give him the encouragement that drove him on to make *Farnborough* one of the most famous of all the Q-ships.

Queenstown was an ideal base for Q-ship operations for it was on the doorstep of the vast area of sea across which the bulk of British merchant shipping travelled. It was commonly known as the Western Approaches and was to be the stamping ground of *Farnborough* throughout most of her career as a Q-ship. It was here that the U-boats concentrated to find rich pickings among the British and Allied merchantmen that plied these waters.

There were certain formalities to be undergone before *Farnborough* could put to sea and while Campbell dealt with those and the final touches were made to his ship, a growing excitement swept through the crew. They were anxious to get to sea and into the fray. At last the night came when *Farnborough* slipped out of Queenstown, to the casual observer a tramp carrying a cargo of coal for some distant destination. It was Campbell's intention to be seen sailing a given course under one identity, then by night change that identity and retrace his steps the following day. By doing this he was less likely to arouse the suspicions of any lurking U-boats. If the same ship were to be seen going back and forth along the same route day after day, any intelligent U-boat commander would tumble to the fact that there was something strange about its behaviour. It was a cunning ruse—and it worked.

But if the crew expected to sail out of Queenstown, lay themselves wide open to attack from the U-boats and quickly score a kill, they were in for a bitter disappointment. Days and nights of cruising the well-plied routes brought no sign of an enemy submarine and Campbell could sense boredom setting in among the crew. He knew they had to play a waiting game, but the crew was not quite so ready to accept this. They wanted action—anything to relieve the tedium of sailing day after day without sight or sound of an enemy. Reports flooded in of British ships being sunk in the area but, try as he might, Campbell could not attract a U-boat to take the bait, despite the fact that, more than once, ships were sunk within only a few miles of his position. He began to wonder if the U-boat commanders had penetrated his disguise. If they had, they might be inclined to give him a wide berth. He scrutinised his camouflage but could find nothing which might betray *Farnborough* as being a Q-ship. Indeed his faith in the disguise was vindicated when he 'passed inspection' not only by other British merchant ships but also by Naval warships, both at sea and in harbour where anyone had a perfect opportunity of giving the ship the once over. It seemed that his 'cover' was perfect. Then why no U-boats? He was a sitting duck but none would take the bait.

Between November 1915 and February 1916, he continued his cruising, breaking the monotony by insisting upon daily drills. After three months of this, the men began to despair that they would ever tangle with a U-boat. The same tedious routines were practised every day and in spite of their efforts to keep up morale, it was on the wane. They were not to know it then, but Campbell's strict discipline and martinet-like approach to training was to bring them their long sought-after prize.

Farnborough put out of Queenstown in mid-March after a short stay to pick up provisions and give the crew some shore leave. She had hardly nosed out of harbour when her wireless fairly crackled with a string of SOS signals from ships in distress. The cries for help came from ships which were either under attack by shell fire or had been torpedoed. It seemed that the U-boats were out in force. To maintain his crew's interest, Campbell made a point of keeping them abreast of developments and he reported the distress signals to them. It was therefore with renewed heart that they began their cruise. Perhaps this time they would be lucky and Campbell was determined to try every trick in the book to catch himself a submarine. He even went to the extent of pretending to be disabled and out of control, remaining stationary and sending signals to fictitious owners asking for help and giving his exact position. Alas even that brought no reward, so on they sailed—and sailed—and sailed. Nothing. Nothing, that is, until at 0640 hours on 22 March, 1916, while steaming north off the west coast of Ireland, the lookout on the port side sighted 'something' about five miles off the port bow. Campbell raised his glass to his eyes and focused on it. Since it was only half light it was difficult to be absolutely certain what the craft was. It could at that distance simply be a fishing vessel going about her lawful and innocent business. But on the other hand it could be a submarine. Campbell watched it intently for several minutes, straining his eyes. Still he could not make up his mind. But then the craft disappeared. Now there was no doubt. She was a submarine which had been riding on the surface and had now submerged. At last, Campbell thought, their chance had come. But there was no guarantee that she would attack or even that the *Farnborough* had been spotted. There was however a distinct possibility that all the drills, all the tactics Campbell had evolved would soon be put into practice.

Above all, he must make no attempt to 'run for it'. He assumed that the submarine's captain would reckon that he had not been seen so Campbell kept *Farnborough* on the same course but by now his guns crews were darting to action stations. Guns were loaded ready for action and the deck crew carried on as usual as if nothing had happened.

Now came the agonising wait to see if an attack would come and, if it did, whether it would be by gun or torpedo. The tension on the boat was electric. The minutes ticked by with painful slowness. But Campbell's discipline was paying off. The deck crew lounged about, some smoking, others dawdling around the deck, not even venturing a glance in the direction of the submarine's last known position. It seemed an age before at last the ominous trail of bubbles zipped towards the tramp steamer. No one on board moved or paid the least attention to it although they all knew by now that it was coming. On it forged lancing through the water only just beneath the surface. Muscles were taut waiting for the inevitable explosion but it did not come. The torpedo shot past the bows of the steamer and the trail of bubbles disappeared. Still no-one showed any sign of having seen the torpedo and Campbell kept the steamer on the same course, praying that the U-boat commander, assuming they had not seen the tin fish, would surface to attack by gun fire.

Meanwhile, Campbell reported to the gun crews and the crew below decks in the engine room that the torpedo had missed. It was they, concealed in the bowels of the ship, who had to suffer the greatest agony for they could see nothing of what was happening. Only the calm voice of their captain kept them in the picture.

On the bridge, Campbell surreptitiously kept an eagle-eyed watch on the sea. Then suddenly the surface exploded in a frothing bubbling turmoil as the submarine broke surface off the port beam. Campbell watched as the U-boat's gun crews spilled out of the hatch and manned the gun. Moments later a shell arced through the sky and whirred across *Farnborough*'s bows to land on her starboard side with a great splash. This was the warning to stop immediately. Campbell obeyed but as *Farnborough* slowed to a halt, the submarine sank into the water, leaving only her conning tower exposed, clearly ready to crash dive if danger threatened. This commander was taking no chances. He was the cautious type.

The drama on the steamer commenced with practised skill while Campbell let off steam. Men darted here and there in a frenzy to reach the boats. They bumped into each other, cursed and swore. Some would appear on deck, then disappear to rescue precious possessions and re-appear on deck. While this was going on, Campbell could feel the U-boat commander's periscope examining the ship, searching for anything unusual about the tramp. Campbell wondered if he already knew of the existence of Q-ships and was searching for a flaw in *Farnborough*'s disguise.

A moment later the submarine came fully to the surface, her hatches were cast open and the deck crew scrambled out of the hatches to man the gun while the captain and other officers filled the conning tower. The U-boat was a mere 800 yards off the port beam now and it was clear to Campbell that his opposite number had taken the bait. The submarine's gun belched fire and a shell narrowly missed the steamer, landing only feet away from her magazine. Had it hit, *Farnborough* would undoubtedly have been no more.

Still the panic party continued their play acting, now with increased fervour. Campbell's eyes were fixed on the submarine, now lying exposed and beam-on to the steamer. Now was the time to strike. Campbell gave the order. The side ports fell away, the hen coop collapsed and the White Ensign fluttered at the masthead. *Farnborough* had shed her veil and within seconds the first rounds were whistling towards the submarine. She was taken completely by surprise. The Maxim gun and rifle fire sprayed the deck, taking their toll of the guns crew while the shells found their mark. In all twenty one shells were fired, most of them scoring hits on the U-boat and puncturing her casing. Now the chaos was transferred from the steamer to the U-boat as men fought to get back inside her and submerge. The water cast up by the shells shrouded the target as she sought succour in the depths. Soon she was gone. Campbell ordered the cease fire and brought *Farnborough* round to charge towards the U-boat's position. Once there, he dropped depth charges which cast towering columns of water high into the air. Then he waited, waited for the sign that the submarine was doomed. The minutes went by, then the flotsam found its way to the surface amid a wide patch of thick black oil. U-68's hunting days were over. She and all her crew had perished. *Farnborough* had scored her first victory, without a single casualty to herself. She had broken her duck. The action had lasted one hour and five minutes.

Campbell signalled Bayly of his success and was ordered back to Queenstown for a well-earned rest. But this was one order Campbell chose to ignore and he continued cruising, seeking further fodder. When he eventually returned to base, he learned that he had been promoted to the rank of Commander and had been admitted to the Distinguished Service Order. In addition, Beswick and Loveless were awarded the Distinguished Service Cross. As a token of their appreciation, the Admiralty awarded the ship £1,000 to be divided among the crew.

Campbell may have 'broken his duck' but it was to be almost a year later before he and the *Farnborough* would be batting again; a year in which the Q-ship was to ply the ocean lanes, offering herself as a victim—but there were no takers. There were minor scuffles but another victory eluded them. Throughout that year, however, a major change took place which was to make their business infinitely more hazardous than it had previously been. The Germans discovered the existence of the Q-ships. The secret was out and now no chances would be taken by the U-boat commanders. It was following this disclosure that Campbell's most glorious encounters took place. By comparison with those which were to come, the sinking of the U-68 was a walk-over.

Having suffered the rigours of Atlantic weather since her commissioning, the time came in January 1917 for *Farnborough* to put into dock for a refit. It was then that Campbell could 'relax' away from the hazard of playing sitting duck to the German submarine service. But his period of respite was not spent enjoying the fruits of an earned rest. The change in the situation at sea and the increasingly devastating effect the U-boats were having upon British and Allied shipping in the Atlantic occupied his mind and he was very anxious to improve *Farnborough*'s effectiveness. He decided upon tactics which were suicidal.

In the action during which U-68 had been sunk, the U-boat's torpedo had missed. It had been seen at some distance and avoiding action could well have been taken. Throughout the year that had just passed, torpedo attacks had been made on *Farnborough* and had missed with the result that the U-boat commander had given up, not being prepared to waste another 'fish' on an unimportant target. Now Campbell proposed revolutionary tactics. On their next foray he decided that if a torpedo were fired at *Farnborough*, he would purposely alter course so that it would hit the ship! This, he reasoned, would be bound to draw the submarine to the surface and allow him to carry out an attack on it. There was of course the possibility that, if the torpedo hit the ship in the magazine, she would be blown to bits. That, Campbell explained to his crew, was a risk he was prepared to take. The question was, would his crew share that suicidal possibility? He put it to them, explaining that anyone who felt he did not want to sail under these conditions was at liberty to leave and nothing less would be thought of him. Not a single man opted to leave. It was both a tribute to Campbell's leadership and the hallmark of the incredible courage of his crew.

In February of that year, the German submarine onslaught intensified and the Western Approaches became the graveyard of thousands of tons of British shipping. As news of the massive losses reached Campbell, his anger grew and he cut every corner to get the refit completed.

By the beginning of February the *Farnborough* was ready and Campbell left port. His orders were to remain at sea for ten days. This was the customary cruise length, but he had sufficient coal on board to remain at sea for at least twenty days and in the first ten days had no sight of a submarine, so he decided to stay longer. His wireless was abuzz with cries for help from stricken merchantmen. To his disgust, Campbell had seen an ammunition ship explode in a great ball of fire not far from his position. He had actually sighted the submarine's periscope not far off his own beam but although the German commander gave the *Farn-*

borough the 'once-over', he decided not to attack. Campbell was furious and his resolution to sink another U-boat increased.

It was on the evening of 16 February that he got his first hint that something was brewing which might bring him a bag. His wireless operator picked up two German submarines communicating with each other. They were close by, so Campbell began his yo-yo style cruising, remaining in the area in the hope that he might make himself the target for a German torpedo.

The night dragged ponderously by with everyone on board keyed-up in anticipation. Dawn came and with it a flat, calm sea beneath a clear blue sky. There was a distinctly pacific air, but it proved to be the calm before the storm. At precisely 0945 hours the mill pond was disturbed by the bubbling track of a torpedo slicing through the water off the starboard beam. She had been spotted and the torpedo fired from quite some distance. Campbell could easily have taken avoiding action. There was plenty of time; nevertheless he allowed the ship to continue on its course. He watched the 'tin fish' as it continued to trace a course towards *Farnborough*. It would just miss the steamer if she held her present course so, with only a fraction of a minute to go, Campbell put the helm over so that the torpedo struck abaft the engine room as he was shouting the last of his orders. It rammed the ship and exploded, tearing a gaping hole in her side, smashing a bulkhead and flooding a good two-thirds of the steamer. On deck the panic party sprang into action while below decks men fought for their lives against the water which gushed in. The engine room had taken the worst of it and was completely swamped. *Farnborough* seemed doomed, and it appeared that there might not be time to attack the submarine if she did show herself.

The panic party's act became a reality as the ship began to settle down at the stern. Campbell, prone on the bridge, squirmed about peering through the slits to catch sight of the submarine's periscope if it should show itself. The delaying tactics employed by the panic party were something to behold as they fumbled about the deck. Some lifeboats jammed, others tipped their human contents into the sea. Seamen were leaping straight into the briny. While the drama unfolded on deck, gun crews stood ready at their weapons, unaware just how perilous their position was.

Meanwhile the plight of the men in the engine and boiler room was becoming dangerous and by voice pipe Campbell ordered them to evacuate it and lie hidden. They dared not come on deck lest they should be seen by the U-boat commander.

Campbell spotted the periscope jutting out of the green and watched it move slowly towards the lifeboats as they pulled away from the ship. It drew closer and closer to the boat that contained the 'ship's master', clearly intending to surface and demand the ship's papers before sinking *Farnborough*. In times of tension like these there is very often a comic element. There was one joker on the boat who, observing the periscope barely ten yards away, warned his mates not to talk too loudly lest the German crew should hear them!

The eye of the periscope carefully examined the men huddled in the lifeboat before turning its attention to the ship, now even lower in the water. Still no-one showed himself. This was the telling time. No-one on board dared to move. The U-boat commander, aware that *Farnborough* might be a Q-ship, was taking no chances. He closed to within fifteen yards of the ship. By then he could clearly see every rivet in her hull and it was now that the whole disguise had to hold up to inspection. The submarine was so close that from his vantage point on the bridge Campbell could see her entire hull just beneath the surface of the water. He felt exposed, naked, and sure that the German would find some tiny flaw that would prompt him to put another torpedo into her, then machine-gun the survivors in the boats.

Campbell was tempted to open fire at the periscope but that would have been a fruitless exercise. No; he had to play the waiting game, praying every moment that none of the crew left on board would show themselves. It was the greatest test of a man's nerves to ask him to remain absolutely still at his post while the ship was sinking beneath his feet. Their lives were in Campbell's hands and they held on to his every quietly-spoken word, as he told them through the voice pipes what was happening outside. The gun position at the stern of the ship had sunk to such an extent that the men operating the gun found their feet awash, but still they held steady for they knew, as did every other man on that steamer, that if they moved into view the entire operation would be a failure, and the result could be a hellish onslaught by the submarine.

Still the submarine did not surface. She slid up the starboard

beam, then crossed the bows, all the time with her commander in-
specting the ship through the periscope. Campbell crawled across
the deck of the bridge to the slits on the port side and saw the submarine's periscope reappear on the port bow, where it stopped. It
was not the best of positions, for if the submarine remained in that
position and surfaced Campbell would not be able to bring his
most powerful guns to bear on her. He willed her to move, and she
did—just a little farther, until she suddenly broke surface about
300 yards off the port beam.

The men in the lifeboats, sensing that the submarine had not
been in the best position, had manoeuvred around to the port
beam where they waited for her to surface and demand the ship's
papers. It later transpired that this was indeed what the submarine
commander had in mind. He was never to get these papers. He
was instead to get the shock of his life.

The hatch in the U-boat's conning tower opened and the commander came onto the bridge. At 1010 hours precisely, Campbell
gave the order to open fire. Down came the flaps and the guns
blazed in a crushing broadside. Almost every one of the forty-five
shells fired from the 12- and 6-pounder guns hit the submarine.
The commander fell back down the conning tower hatch and the
crew began to appear on deck as the boat was ripped apart. The
gaping perforations in the submarine's casing transformed her
into a sieve through which the sea poured in. Her conning tower
became a tangled wreck and, of her entire crew, only about eight
managed to squirm out of the boat and into a sea now calmed by a
thick coating of lethal oil. The oil was gulped in by them, filling
their lungs, and they slid beneath the waves to a sailor's grave.
Only two survivors, an officer and a rating, were rescued by the
panic party's boats. Doomed, U-83 went down in a bubbling turmoil. *Farnborough* had claimed her second victim.

However, with the submarine dispatched to the depths, it
looked as if *Farnborough* might well follow. She was two-thirds
flooded and sinking at the stern. Now, after that agonising wait,
the wireless operator who until then had been forbidden to send
out a distress signal, tapped out an SOS while the panic party
reboarded the ship.

Everyone set to with a will to save the ship, but despite all their
efforts, it was clear to Campbell that if help did not come soon
Farnborough would sink. He therefore ordered all but twelve

volunteers to take to the boats and stand off lest she should sink suddenly. As the minutes became hours and no sign came of rescue ships, it seemed that this would be the end of the *Farnborough*. The wireless officer continued to send out distress signals until at last Campbell sent a signal to the C-in-C, Admiral Bayly: 'Q5 (*Farnborough*) slowly sinking respectfully wishes you goodbye'.

Campbell ditched all the confidential papers and the safe in which records of their cruises were kept. Secret charts were burnt and all prepared for what seemed an inevitable fate. The lifeboats stood by to take off Campbell and the twelve men still on board. But at noon smoke was sighted on the horizon. The destroyer *Narwhal* was racing to their aid, closely followed by HMS *Buttercup*. The latter took *Farnborough* in tow, but the tow soon parted and had to be refixed. It was not until 1700 hours, seven hours after the torpedo had struck, that the two finally got under way. *Farnborough* was now very low in the water and it was doubtful that she would make land but thanks to the great seamanship of the crew of *Buttercup*, the tow continued. Suddenly, however, there was an almighty explosion. One of the depth charges had inexplicably blown up. Surely now *Farnborough* must sink completely. Yet the determined old tramp did not intend to give up, despite having taken on a 20-degree list. It was by now pitch dark, the time being 0330 hours. Campbell decided that this was the time to abandon her and he and the others who had courageously remained with him left the ship.

Much to their surprise, *Farnborough* did not disappear beneath the waves, and when dawn came she was still there, drifting derelict without a tow. The resilient old tramp would not be defeated. She was taken in tow once more and after a game fight was beached on the coast of Ireland.

Farnborough was finished as a Q-ship, but the spirited old steamer's life at sea was not over. After she had been cannibalised by Campbell, who retrieved all her guns, she was refloated, refitted and put to sea again as a tramp until she was eventually broken up for scrap. Campbell was presented with the ship's bell, but that was not his only award. For the action in which he sank the U-83, he was awarded the Victoria Cross, his country's highest medal for valour. Among the honours bestowed upon the crew were two DSOs, three DSCs and ten DSMs. Twenty-four others were Mentioned in Dispatches. In addition to this, £1,000 was again awarded to be divided among the crew.

Campbell now found himself without a command, so he set about selecting another tramp for the purpose. He went to Cardiff docks where he found just the ship he had been looking for, a collier of 2,635 tons. He lost no time in laying claim to her and she was quickly fitted out in her new role as a Q-ship. There were some additions to the facilities the old *Farnborough* had had. Besides a four-inch gun, three twelve-pounders and depth charges, Campbell had two torpedo tubes installed, one on either side of the ship, which could be fired through hidden ports. The ship was renamed *Pargust*. Like *Farnborough* she was destined for great things which were not to be achieved without great danger.

She had not long to wait for action. At the end of May, 1917, *Pargust* was steaming off the coast of Ireland when she was struck by a torpedo. The weather was appalling, but despite the heavy seas and thick mist the torpedo found its mark, smack in the engine room. It ripped a forty-foot wide hole in the ship's side and the engine room was completely flooded. The explosion wrecked the lifeboat on the starboard side, leaving only one lifeboat and two rafts for the panic party. They boarded these, and as they were pulling away they spotted the submarine's periscope about 400 yards off the port side. She was moving closer to the torpedoed ship for an inspection and got within 40 feet, scanning the ship through the 'scope. It was plain that the commander was unsure what he had torpedoed and he began a series of circular courses at periscope depth, scrutinising the ship and the men in the boats until finally he surfaced, but in the most awkward position, off the port quarter where Campbell could not get the maximum number of guns trained on him. All remained still on the *Pargust* but in the boat Hereford, who was acting as ship's master, saw Campbell's predicament and ordered his oarsmen to pull the boats round to the starboard side of the ship, hoping the submarine would follow. She did this, trailing the boats as they rounded *Pargust*'s stern. When the boats were amidships of *Pargust* and the submarine off their beam, Hereford pulled towards the steamer to give Campbell a clear field of fire. But Campbell had a few moments to wait until the commander of the U-boat opened the hatch. Clearly, the German was becoming annoyed at Hereford's unwillingness to stay still. This was precisely what Hereford had wanted and, with the submarine now showing her full length to the Q-ship, the commander opened the hatch and produced a loud hailer. He had uttered only a few words when all hell was let loose. Campbell had chosen his moment with sheer perfection and the submarine took the full weight of the Q-ship's broadside at a distance of only 50 yards. The guns peppered the submarine with fire while a torpedo was loosed at her, but it missed. The hail of gunfire continued, shattering the conning tower while rifle fire took its toll of German sailors who spilled out on to the deck to man their gun. Their attempt was in vain. Soon the after hatch of the submarine was opened and some more of the crew revealed themselves with their arms held in the air. Campbell ordered 'cease fire'. It appeared that the submarine had surrendered. But suddenly she put on a burst of speed in a bid to escape into the mist. Campbell had no alternative but to open fire again while the German crew on the deck were washed into the sea. Only a few more shots were fired before there was a violent explosion in the submarine and she sank. Campbell had claimed another victim and the panic party picked up what German survivors there were.

Pargust, her engines out of action, was helpless and had to call for aid. Luckily she remained afloat and was towed back to Queenstown.

It was only after the action that Campbell learned of the momentous acts of courage which had taken place onboard *Pargust* during her encounter with the U-boat. Several of the men who were to man one of the deck guns had had to lie motionless on the deck throughout the agonising half hour after the torpedo had struck. Had they moved, the game would have been up. The impact of the torpedo and the resulting explosion had dislodged one of the flaps hiding a gun and Able Seaman William Williams had put his back to the heavy metal flap and held it in position until the order to fire came. Had it fallen away the gun would have been exposed, with obvious results.

Every single man on that ship had shown immense courage and it was decided that two Victoria Crosses should be awarded to the ship. A secret ballot was held by the crew and the two medals were awarded to Lieutenant Neil Stuart and Seaman William Williams. Campbell was promoted to Captain and awarded a bar to his DSO. Almost every other member of the crew was decorated.

It might be thought that Campbell and his crew had more than 'done their bit', but they were by no means finished. With *Pargust* out of action and under repair, Campbell went to look for a third Q-ship. Alas when he next encountered a U-boat and engaged her in action, the U-boat won the day. His new Q-ship, the *Dunraven*, was sunk when her magazine exploded, but not before Campbell and his crew had put up yet another epic fight. This classic action was described in the London Gazette in November 1918. It read:

'On the 8th August, 1917, HMS *Dunraven* under the command of Captain Gordon Campbell VC, DSO, RN, sighted an enemy submarine on the horizon. In her role of armed British merchant ship, the *Dunraven* continued her zig-zag course, whereupon the submarine closed, remaining submerged to within 5,000 yards, and then, rising to the surface, opened fire. The *Dunraven* returned the fire with her merchant ship gun, at the same time reducing speed to enable the enemy to overtake her. Wireless signals were also sent out for the benefit of the submarine: "Help! Come quickly—submarine chasing and shelling me." Finally, when the shells began falling close, the *Dunraven* stopped and abandoned ship by the 'panic party'. The ship was then being heavily shelled, and on fire aft. In the meantime, the submarine closed to 400 yards distant, partly obscured from view by the dense clouds of smoke issuing from the *Dunraven*'s stern. Despite the knowledge that the after-magazine must inevitably explode if he waited, and further, that a gun and gun crew lay concealed over the magazine, Captain Campbell decided to reserve his fire until the submarine had passed clear of the smoke. A moment later, however, a heavy explosion occurred aft, blowing the gun and gun crew into the air, and accidentlly starting the fire-gongs at the remaining gun positions; screens were immediately dropped, and the only gun that would bear opened fire, but the submarine, apparently frightened by the explosion, had already commenced to submerge. Realising that a torpedo must inevitably follow, Captain Campbell ordered the surgeon to remove all wounded and conceal them in cabins; hoses were also turned on the poop, which was a mass of flames. A signal was sent out warning men-of-war to divert all traffic below the horizon in order that nothing should interrupt the final phase of the action. Twenty minutes later a torpedo again struck the ship abaft the engine room. An additional party of men were again sent away as a 'panic party' and left the ship to outward appearances completely abandoned, with the White Ensign flying and guns unmasked. For the succeeding fifty minutes the submarine examined the ship through her periscope. During this period boxes of cordite and shells exploded every few minutes, and the fire on the poop still blazed furiously. Captain Campbell and a handful of officers and men who remained on board lay hidden during this ordeal. The submarine then rose to the surface astern, where no guns could bear, and shelled the ship closely for twenty minutes. The enemy then submerged and steamed past the ship 150 yards off, examining her through the periscope. Captain Campbell decided then to fire one of his torpedoes, but missed by a few inches. The submarine crossed the bows and came slowly down the other side, whereupon a second torpedo was fired and missed again. The enemy observed it and immediately submerged. Urgent signals for assistance were immediately sent out, but pending arrival of assistance Captain Campbell arranged for a third 'panic party' to jump overboard if necessary and leave one gun crew on board for a final attempt to destroy the enemy, should he again attack. Almost immediately afterwards, however, British and American destroyers arrived on the scene, the wounded were transferred, boats were recalled, and the fire extinguished. The *Dunraven*, although her stern was awash, was taken in tow, but the weather grew worse, and early the following morning she sank with colours flying.'

Following another ballot, two members of the crew were awarded the Victoria Cross. They were Lieutenant C. G. Bonner and Petty Officer E. Pitcher. Campbell was awarded a further bar to his DSO, making him one of the most highly decorated officers in the Royal Navy.

Campbell's most secret service in 'mystery ships' had won for him and his crew *five* Victoria Crosses and a treasure trove of other awards. His skill and ingenuity in waging his unconventional form of warfare against submarines had resulted in the sinking of three of them. This might not seem an overwhelmingly handsome 'bag', but bearing in mind the immense potential destructive power of a single submarine, one cannot doubt that many lives were saved by Campbell's courageous action.

5

Baltic Episode

Lieutenant Augustus Agar's face creased in an apprehensive, almost nervous smile which was not returned by the attractive young secretary he met at the Admiralty buildings in London. He had finally reached his goal, a blank, unimpressive door at the terminus of a warren of antiseptically white painted corridors. Agar had navigated the maze in the wake of a commander RN, whose athletic pace along the linoleumed labyrinth indicated the urgency of the appointment Agar was about to keep.

Agar sensed he was in alien territory as he stepped through the door held open by the young woman and into a plush suite of offices. The deck of a battleship or the cockpit of one of His Majesty's coastal motor boats, of which he had recently taken command, were more familiar ground. But here he was, a sailor out of water, summoned to the inner sanctum of the British Secret Intelligence Service and about to meet its chief.

The young lieutenant knew little of what lay in store for him, save that he was about to embark upon a top secret mission, the details of which were to be explained to him by Britain's masterspy. The nature of the clandestine mission had been vaguely explained to Agar only the day before when he was called to a conference with his flotilla commander, Captain Wilfred French. Agar had been ordered to French's cabin, where he found his chief engrossed in studying charts of the Baltic and its environs. French looked up from his desk with furrowed brow.

'Ah, Agar. Just the man. Come in. I have a job for you that I think is just up your street.'

French indicated a chair and Agar sat down while his superior perched himself on the edge of his desk. The Captain did not prevaricate but came straight to the point.

'The cloak and dagger boys at the Foreign Office want two of our CMBs to undertake a special mission in the Baltic. Frankly I don't know what it's all about. It seems that the show is so secret that only a handful of people are to know about it and that doesn't include me.

French paused for a moment to take in Agar's reaction which clearly showed an expression of almost boyish excitement. The Captain knew his man and had expected this.

'I have chosen you to take command of these boats . . .'

There seemed to be no question of French asking Agar to volunteer for the adventure, as was the usual form in cases such as this. There had never been any doubt in the captain's mind about Agar's willingness to take on this special duty. It was 1919 and the Great War had been over for almost a year. Agar was restless in his peacetime role in the Navy and French knew that he would jump at the chance to get into action again.

'. . . you will take two of our smallest CMBs, the forty-footers, into the Baltic and operate in the Gulf of Finland,' French went on. 'I must tell you, Agar, that the matter is so secret that you must discuss it with no one, not even your closest colleagues.

'For the purposes of this mission, you will work as a civilian and be directly responsible to the Foreign Office. You will have absolute command of the operation of the boats in the Baltic and no one—*not even the Navy*—must know who you are or what you are doing there. Is that clearly understood?'

Agar could hardly believe his own ears as he nodded in consent to his captain's conditions.

'This has been given top priority,' French added. 'Tomorrow you are to report to Whitehall where you'll be briefed in detail. You'd better get moving. You'll want to put your things in order before getting too involved in all this. Off you go then. And, Agar—good luck.'

'Thank you, sir.'

Agar rose from his seat, saluted and left, leaving French to his charts. Outside, the noise and clatter of the CMB base on Osea Island, which lay in a remote corner of Essex, went unheard by Agar as he strode towards his quarters, deep in thought. His mind was buzzing at the prospect of the new appointment. Without his knowing anything of it, the Secret Intelligence Service had selected him for this task which carried the mark of a spy thriller. It was while considering this that an incident which had occurred only a few days before came to mind. He recalled that it had struck him as a little odd at the time.

An elderly man wearing the uniform of a naval captain had arrived at Osea Island one morning and was taken on a tour of inspection. He showed keen interest in the CMBs and plied Agar with searching questions about their capabilities. There was nothing new or unusual about this. Visits were quite frequent. After all, Agar mused, senior officers had to find something to do and snap inspections seemed as good a way as any of working out their time till retirement.

This particular captain struck Agar as long overdue for the breaker's yard. He wore a monocle and walked with a pronounced limp, supporting himself by means of a stout stick. But as the tour of inspection continued, Agar became aware that there might be more to this old sea dog than his appearance might suggest. He had about him an intensity of thought and purpose that impressed Agar. When the tour ended, the old salt thanked Agar and expressed the hope that they would meet again. Agar had no idea of it then but the captain had come to inspect not only the boats, but him too.

Agar continued towards his quarters, past the CMBs moored side by side at piers like piglets at a sow's paps. As he did so, he reflected upon the sketchy details French had given him. Why, he wondered, did the Secret Service want CMBs? What role could they possibly play in the Baltic and why on earth had they chosen him for the task?

The Coastal Motor Boat (CMB) was the smallest offensive surface craft in service with the Royal Navy and Agar was a comparative newcomer to it. It was the brainchild of a group of naval officers who had been given the task of designing a small, fast torpedo carrying craft. The boat that emerged as the First World War was drawing to a close, was the CMB, the fore-runner of the Motor Torpedo Boat, which later figured so prominently in the Second World War.

The CMBs were small and fast, ranging in length from 40 to 55 feet. The smaller of the two carried one torpedo, while the larger model was equipped with two torpedoes with which to attack enemy warships. Even when fully loaded, they could skim across the water at speeds up to 40 knots which gave them a dash resembling that of the air force fighter challenging an enemy bomber. They carried their sting in their backsides. The torpedo lay in a trough and was fired over the stern which meant turning their backs on the enemy to loose the 'fish' at the target. This method of launching had the advantage of allowing the CMB to escape the immediate danger area while the torpedo was coursing through the water en route for the enemy ship.

The three-man crew of the CMB occupied the cramped, open cockpit amidships and had to brave the elements with no cover to protect them. The spray cast up from the bows invariably soaked the crew, making it a very uncomfortable way of going to war. Despite this, they provided the war chariots in which two sailors won the Victoria Cross during the epic Zeebrugge raid in 1918 when an attempt was made to block the canal along which German U-boats were finding their exits to the North Sea.

The CMBs were specifically designed to attack enemy ships lying at anchor in areas like the Terscheeling Roads and other German anchorages. CMB bases were quickly established along the south and east coasts of England, including the one at Osea Island, to which Agar was assigned. But his duty was to be somewhat different from that of the conventional CMB. His boats were designed for mine-laying and it was proposed that even bigger 70-footers would come into service equipped to carry and lay the new magnetic mines which were just becoming available.

But first Agar had to master the eccentricities of the CMB. To this end, he went to both Dover and Dunkirk, spending time with experienced CMB officers who could show him the ropes. Then from there he was despatched to the Royal Navy's Torpedo School, there to learn the techniques of mine-laying and particularly that of laying the new magnetic mine. Upon his return to Osea Island, French promised him command of a CMB flotilla.

Agar's first taste of action in CMBs came on the eve of Armistice and resulted in a complete debacle. The boats were towed across the Channel and slipped off near the Heligoland Bight. Bad planning and inexperience made the operation fruitless and when the boats attempted to rejoin their tow ships, they missed them. The six CMBs made a bid to re-cross the sea to England but in doing so came under attack from German fighter aircraft. All six boats were machine-gunned and badly holed. Some of the boats struggled back but the others drifted hopelessly towards Holland and their crews were captured and interned for the remainder of the war. Agar learned of his comrades' fate when carrier pigeons which had been released from the stricken boats arrived back at Osea Island.

The Armistice was signed before the Osea base became fully operational and there were fears that her flotillas would be disbanded. But there were jobs for her boats in warmer climes and French and Agar set about building up the strength for overseas duties. In addition, Agar was given the unenviable task of sweeping mines which had been laid in vast fields across the North Sea.

His summons to Whitehall that day in the Spring of 1919 came as a welcome, if mysterious, break from the tedium of minesweeping. So it was that he presented himself at the nerve-centre of the British Secret Intelligence Service . . .

The Commander from Naval Intelligence drew the secretary aside and a whispered conference was held out of Agar's hearing. A few moments later they broke the clinch and the secretary pointed to a door.

'You are wanted in there, Lieutenant. Please go straight in.'

With that Agar strode forward, clasped the door handle in his hand, turned it and pushed it. The door opened to his thrust, revealing a large room, with a vast wooden desk at its far side. Agar was about to step in when his eyes caught sight of the man seated at the desk. Recognition was instant. There was no mistaking the monocle and the round, lined face with its penetrating eyes. Here was the naval captain who had shown such interest in Agar's CMBs. But now he wore civilian clothes. Was this ageing mariner the brains behind Britain's Secret Service, Agar thought as he closed the door behind himself.

The captain was intent upon the mound of papers on his desk. He continued to read while Agar hovered self-consciously at the door, wondering what on earth he should do. As if in answer to his unspoken question, the captain lifted his head.

'Ah, come in, my boy. Take a seat. Make yourself comfortable. Shan't be a moment. Got to wade through mountains of this gubbins even in my line of business, you know.'

He fell silent once more and returned to his papers while Agar found a chair and sat patiently waiting.

The greying, monocled gentleman so intent upon his papers was Captain Mansfield Cumming, chief of the British Secret Service. Because of the Service's mania for anonimity, Mansfield was known cryptically as 'C'. He was one of the most picturesque characters in the Secret Service and had become something of a legendary figure, known for his unorthodox approach in the selection of agents. While Mansfield's predecessors had opted for academics or men who had a military career behind them, he sought out men who had 'the cut of the gib of an alert agent'. He was a gay dog and had the reputation of being something of a lady's man. Cumming liked his agents to be men of vitality and, unlike previous chiefs, did not frown upon them taking their fair share of life's pleasures.

Cumming was almost obsessive about speed and loved fast cars. It was this passion that brought tragedy to his mercurial life. The car in which he and his son were travelling crashed and his son was trapped. One of Cumming's legs was crushed and he is said to have cut it off in a bid to reach and rescue his son. But the boy died before he could get to him.

Cumming was fitted with a wooden leg and this gave him an opportunity of un-nerving prospective agents when they were being interviewed. He took great delight in striking matches on the leg or tapping it with a pen-knife, all guaranteed to raise an eyebrow.

The exuberant spy chief brought a breath of fresh air to the otherwise stuffy hierarchy of the Secret Service and despite his idiosyncrasies is credited with laying the foundations upon which the modern Secret Service is based today.

As if remembering suddenly that he was not alone, Cumming swept aside the papers on his desk and focused his attention upon the young naval lieutenant sitting before him. He smiled, the first hint of friendship Agar had encountered since entering these hallowed halls.

'Well, my boy,' he began with patronising geniality. 'His Majesty's Secret Service has need of your help in a rather delicate operation of the utmost importance—and secrecy. . . .'

Cumming leaned forward on his desk before continuing. With hands clasped before him, he resembled a don about to deliver a lecture. In essence that is what he did, with a monologue of explanation, summarising the political situation that existed in Russia at that time.

Following the Red Revolution, the Bolsheviks had taken control of almost the entire country but they were opposed by the White Russians. The sympathies of the British government lay with the Whites and Britain was actively supporting them, without making their assistance too obvious. Should the extent of Britain's involvement become known, then a full-scale war might ensue, hence the need for absolute secrecy in all their dealings with the Whites.

British spies had penetrated Red Russia and a very effective network of agents had been set up but quite recently there had been a breakdown in communication.

'Our links with our agents in Russia must be restored as quickly as possible,' Cumming said forcefully. 'We have couriers who ferry out information to us from our agents. They're damned courageous people who risk their lives getting that information in and out. If the Bolshies got their hands on them they'd have their guts. These chaps smuggle messages across the frontier into Finland and pass them on to our people there. Well, somewhere along the line, the link in the chain has been broken. You job will be to re-establish that link. I can't tell you how vital it is to our whole espionage operation there.

'Our most important agent there—you will know him simply as ST25— is in Petrograd. He's the best man we've got—but we've lost contact with him. I want him contacted and brought back here to report to me personally. It is crucial to our whole espionage effort in Russia that we know what is going on and only ST25 can put us in the picture. I'm relying on you to get him out. I know your record, Agar, and I'm confident you can do it.'

'I'll do my best, sir,' Agar assured him a trifle meekly.

Cumming went on to explain how he thought it could be done. Fresh couriers would have to slip into Russia and he guessed that Agar's CMBs were best equipped to dash across the Gulf of Finland and put the couriers ashore on the coast of Estonia. From there they would cross the frontier and make their way to Petrograd and explain to ST25 a plan of escape that Agar would devise.

'The fewer people who know what you're up to the better, so I propose telling only the head of your own Naval Intelligence what you're doing and where you're going. Our agents in the Baltic will be briefed and you can count on them for all the help they can give.'

Cumming paused for a moment, as if to allow Agar time to grasp the enormity of the task that faced him and the dangers it was likely to involve. Then, drawing breath, he continued ...

'You'll need a cover for your operation. Obviously you can't wear uniform. You'll be civilians, posing as salesmen for a boat building company. The two boats you take with you are samples, demonstration models if you like.

'Well, that's basically it. I'll leave the selection of crews to you. I suggest you pick 'em young and make damned sure they're as keen as mustard—but above all reliable. Don't want anyone who'll flunk things if you get into a tight corner. That's it then, Agar. Get yourself back to Osea, pick your men and boats, then come back to me when your plans are complete. But make it soon. There's no time to waste.'

Cumming's eyes dropped back towards his papers. The interview was at an end. Agar left. Outside the door he encountered the attractive young secretary once more. This time she managed a faint smile. This, it would appear, was the seal of approval. Agar had joined the élite ranks of the British Secret Service.

Agar emerged from the building, hardly noticing the thin sheets of light rain that bathed the busy London street. He raised an arm in the air and a cab slid to the kerbside in obedience to his command. Agar climbed in, his mind firmly focused upon the myriad problems surrounding the escapade upon which he was about to embark.

The cabbie flicked open the sliding glass window which separated him from his fare. 'Where to, Guv?' he asked.

The chirpy cockney voice jolted Agar from his thoughts.

'Eh—what?' he said absently. 'Oh, sorry, cabbie.' Lost in his thoughts, Agar forgot the name of the railway station he was to head for. Then he remembered and the taxi swept out into the stream of bustling traffic.

Agar settled back into his seat, oblivious to the deft and often hair-raising manoeuvres of the cab as it wound through the traffic.

Throughout the journey back to Osea Island the thought that most occupied his mind was the selection of his crews. He knew all the crews on the island personally and as the train raced through the green and lush countryside, Agar went through them man by man, earmarking one here and there for further consideration; discarding others as unsuitable. By the time the train drew into the station, he had drawn up a short list. He would approach French and finalise the selection.

There was no time to be lost. Spurred on by the thought of ST25 alone in an alien country, cut off from his friends, in constant danger of discovery and death, Agar plunged into the preparations for the mission with a will. He knew that he could count on French's help and his chief, realising that Agar could tell him little of what he was about, submitted to all his requests without question and gave advice whenever he could. First was his request for three officers and two mechanics to make up the crews. He asked for three young sub-lieutenants, Sindall, the eldest, Marshall and Hampshire, all of whom he knew to be keen and able. Then he recruited his mechanics, Beeley and Piper, who were renowned for their intimate knowledge of engines. He could not have chosen a better pair.

In the interest of security, Agar was obliged to withhold from them the truth about the operation. Time did not permit him to concoct a convincing 'blind' to tell the crews. He simply told them that they were to embark upon a mission to reinforce a flotilla overseas. He made no mention of the hazardous nature of the operation or that, if they fell into the hands of the Bolsheviks, they would in all probability be summarily executed. The perils of the expedition would be spelled out to them later—when it was too late to back out. However, in the meantime, the cover story seemed to satisfy their naturally inquisitive minds and they launched themselves into the preparations with gusto.

With his crews selected, and satisfied that he had chosen the right men for the job, Agar turned his attentions to the two boats he would take with him. He chose two of the 40-footers and submitted them to rigorous trials and complete overhauls before finally passing them 'fit' for the operation.

Agar drew up a list of essential stores and when these were amassed, they and the two boats were delivered to the docks in London, ready for shipment. But before being loaded, they were repainted so as to make them unrecognisable as naval craft. After their cosmetic coat of paint they looked exactly like the sort of fast motor boat a wealthy young man might buy for speed racing. Both boats were labelled for delivery to a company of yacht agents in the Finnish coastal town of Abo. Then these and the stores were sunk into the ship's hold, snug and secure, not to see the light of day before arrival in Finland. Their unloading would be left to Cumming's agents in Finland.

With the first stage of the operation complete, Agar once more called upon Cumming. He found him in good spirits and anxious to know how far his plans had advanced. Agar put him in the picture, revealing that he would have to rely upon the agents in Finland to acquire stocks of fuel for the boats. He had made an exhaustive study of the charts of the Gulf of Finland and selected several possible sites for his base from the multitudinous inlets which punctuated the Finnish coastline. The most likely one lay at a point on the coast some 50 miles from Estonia which would mean a voyage of around two hours from the base to the dropping off point for the couriers.

The Chief of the Secret Service had listened to Agar's report without interruption, using his vast experience in these matters to detect flaws, but he found none. Then he leant back in his chair and with a broad grin pronounced his satisfaction.

'You've done well, Agar. I'm pleased. You seem to have thought of everything. There are, however, a couple of other things I must tell you. You appreciate of course that if the Bolshies get their hands on you in civilian clothes on their side of the frontier, they'll have no hesitation in shooting you as a spy. I suggest therefore that each of you takes along a naval uniform which you can put on to prove you are Navy if the need arises. But I must insist that these uniforms are kept in the boats and are never—repeat never—taken out of them.

'One more thing, the moment you board the boat for Finland, you'll assume the false identities we'll provide you with. You'll be given new passports and a complete cover story which you all must learn until it is word perfect. It could mean the difference between life and death for you and your men. You personally, as commander of the unit, will be known to all your contacts and in communications with us as ST34.

'Remember, Agar,' he said sternly, 'you will be on your own. If you get into a mess you'll have to get yourself out of it by your own devices. Our agents will help you if they can but I don't want them put in jeopardy. Apart from the agents, only one more person in the Baltic will know that you are there. He is Admiral Sir Walter Cowan. He's commanding some cruisers and destroyers in these waters.'

Cumming rose from his chair and banged an open hand on the desk, bringing the interview to an end. Then, almost as an afterthought, he added . . .

'Now then, you'll need some money to cover expenses. How much d'you think you'll need?'

Agar hadn't given the question of expenses any thought and blurted out.

'Em, a thousand pounds, I think, sir.'

Cumming, without as much as raising an eyebrow, pressed a buzzer on his desk. The rasping sound summoned his secretary.

'Ah, bring me in a cheque for a thousand pounds and make it payable to cash.'

Without as much as a flutter of surprise on her face, the secretary muttered a 'Very good, sir' and left. Agar, gathering his wits became aware that his mouth was wide open in awe and disbelief. He was aghast at the simplicity with which so much money could be drawn without query.

Cumming went on, 'If you or your men require money for your personal needs you can take it out of the thousand. Of course, it will be regarded as an advance on your pay. Try and keep some account of what you spend. No need to be too particular though. It's an agent we're employing, not an accountant. If you run out of cash and want more you need only ask one of your contacts and he'll get it for you.'

At that the secretary returned with the cheque duly drawn up and handed it to Cumming who passed it on to Agar. The young lieutenant had never handled so much money and for a moment—only a moment—he felt like a millionaire. But the thought of carrying the responsibility for so much cash brought a frown to his face.

'Don't look so worried, Agar—it won't bounce!' Cumming said with a grin. 'That's it for the moment then. My secretary here will take you to get your passports and other bits and pieces. You'll have lunch with me at my club tomorrow. An unofficial affair, you realise. Think of it as a last supper, eh, what?' Cumming bellowed in hearty appreciation of his own humour. Agar forced an apprehensive chuckle then left with the secretary.

The fledgeling spy was shepherded through the honeycomb of passages to a room where he was presented with all the paraphernalia essential to an espionage operation: false passports, codes names, ciphers, lists of contacts known only by their code names, emergency procedures and invisible inks. The last details of departure for and arrival in Finland were explained to him. All this he had to commit to memory then, with his mind abuzz with all this information, he left the headquarters building for the last time before the mission.

That night he lay awake in bed, unable to sleep. His mind was filled with the myriad details he had to memorise. There was only forty-eight hours left before he was due to depart and his mind was haunted by the thought that he might have overlooked some vital point. At last, sheer mental exhaustion overtook him and he lapsed into unconsciousness.

At noon the following day he presented himself at Cumming's club in central London. His chief was in jovial mood, no doubt masking the feeling that he might well be sending this young man and his comrades to their deaths. Cumming had done this many times before—and on some occasions his worst fears had been realised when agents had disappeared without trace. The burden of this responsibility weighed heavily upon him but he never showed it; the gay, colourful exterior hid that.

Cumming was in excellent form and recited for his guest a fascinating monologue of his personal experiences. There was no talk of spies or of Agar's impending adventure. He was bent on giving his new recruit a splendid send-off and he more than fulfilled that objective. The meal was superb and the dialogue complemented it to make the lunch a memorable experience for Agar. He was to think back on it many times during the difficult and hazardous days that lay ahead.

At last Cumming intimated that he would have to leave. He accompanied Agar to the door of the club then turned to him and forced a smile.

'Good luck, my boy.' With that he walked off and was gone. Agar was destined to act out the greatest adventure of his life before they would meet again.

The following day Agar, Hampsheir and Beeley made their way to where a grubby Swedish cargo ship was berthed at the docks. They would make their way to Finland and be followed a week later by Sindall, Marshall and Piper who were to accompany the CMBs.

The ship's master had the stamp of a man who had spent his entire life on the water—but never in it. His attire blended like a chameleon with the tatty and rusty ship. However, he magnanimously gave over his seedy quarters to the three passengers—but not before Agar had dipped deep into the coffers and crossed the old salt's greasy palm with silver.

In due course the ship cast off and, much to the amazement of the three British sailors, got under way. It became clear that 'swabbing the decks' was not one of the daily routines aboard this pleasure craft and she certainly looked as if she had not had a coat of paint since her launching, whenever that might have been. But, despite the disagreeable surroundings and ever-present feeling that all three would soon be consigned to the deep, Agar and his two companions succeeded in concentrating their thoughts upon the task that lay ahead.

Now that they were clear of England's shores, Agar felt free to enlighten the others about the true purpose of their mission. As he had predicted, the prospect of their new assignment was met with great enthusiasm and excitement. He pointed out that Finland was neutral in its feelings towards both Russia and Britain and favoured neither side. So they would have to tread very warily when they arrived on Finnish soil. Exposure of their true intent could—and indeed would—ruin the entire operation and undoubtedly cause an international incident which would cause considerable embarrassment to His Majesty's government. They would have to make themselves as inconspicuous as possible and ensure that their cover story was not 'blown'. A false move, a wrong word, could bring about disaster.

With Agar's warning ringing in their ears they landed in Finland. It occurred to them that the dangers into which they were stepping might well be preferable to those which they had just endured in the rusty old tub which had borne them across the sea.

Agar made directly for Helsinki where he made immediate contact with two of Cumming's agents, ST30 and ST31. They welcomed him warmly and although they had been forewarned of his arrival, neither of them knew what he was to do in Finland—another example of Cumming's caution. Agar's most urgent priority was to find a temporary base from which he could organise the setting up of a permanent station for his boats. The agents soon found him and the two others comfortable rooms in a lodging house where the beds had soft, luxuriously clean sheets. The experience of lying between these was almost heavenly after their ten-day ordeal in a tossing and pitching bunk aboard the Swedish ship. After a refreshing night's sleep, the three Britons became locked in debate over the setting up of the CMB base. They had only a week in which to finally select a venue before the boats were due to arrive. Choosing the right place was of paramount importance. Agar had ear-marked several possible sites before leaving England and now each of them would have to be surveyed for suitability.

It was during this intense debate that another of Cumming's agents made an appearance at their lodgings. He was destined to play a leading role in the drama that was about to unfold.

(In his later accounts of these events, Agar gives this newcomer the cover name of 'Peter' and does not reveal his true identity. It is likely however that he was an ex-Russian Army officer, Kolya Orlov, who had worked closely with ST25 in Russia. Since there is still some doubt as to his real identity, I shall refer to him as 'O'.)

'O' was a courier and had penetrated the frontier many times, carrying information in and out. He more than fitted Cumming's 'cut of the jib of a secret agent'; a flamboyant character imbued with unshakeable nerves. The adrenalin pumped fast in 'O' and one could sense a powerful force inside him that craved the excitement and tension of danger. His knowledge of the English language was all but non-existent and likewise Agar's Russian was restricted to elementary phrases. But the lack of fluent dialogue did nothing to prevent the two men striking up an immediate friendship which was to stand the test of some moments of great danger.

ST31 acted as interpreter and through him 'O' mentioned in passing that he had 'acquired' some top secret Russian charts which might be of some use to 'Egger', as he called him. He made no mention of how he had come by them and no amount of prompting would induce him to reveal his method. The folded sheets of paper he handed to 'Egger' were priceless. Agar could hardly believe his eyes when he scanned the charts. The agent had not only presented him with a detailed map of the entire defence system around and in the approaches of Petrograd but, Agar was quick to see, a possible route for the couriers into Russia. He was speechless.

When 'O' finally left, Agar retired to his room and spent the remainder of the night poring over the charts. The great city of Petrograd lay at the very extremity of the Gulf of Finland. At this point the Gulf narrows to some twenty miles in width and is the only sea route to the city. Sitting large and menacing in this neck of water is the island of Kronstadt, standing as a natural defensive fortress against sea attack upon the city. On either side of the island stood a string of fortresses linking the island with the north and south shores. To add further to the impenetrability of the approaches, the Russians had sunk breakwaters between each of the forts and these were sunk at a depth of three feet beneath the surface of the water.

On the face of it there seemed no way in to Petrograd with these tight defences. But the breakwaters which would certainly impede the passage of large boats and ships posed no barrier for Agar's CMBs which could skim across the water with their shallow draught. Minefields proliferated in the wide canyon of water but since they were laid deep to catch the hulls of large ships they were no problem for the CMBs which could skate across them with impunity.

The germ of an idea was growing in Agar's mind. He might, he thought, just have the answer to the problem of getting the couriers into Russia. His original plan had been to land them on the Estonian coast and from there they would travel overland into Russia, a dangerous and exhausting trek with the perils of crossing the frontier facing them. But Agar now saw a way of taking them right into Russia itself, at the very doorstep of Petrograd. Searching the chart he became more and more convinced of the feasibility of his plan.

'Damn it!' he thought. 'It can be done but I'll need the help of someone who knows these waters well, someone like a fisherman—or better still a smuggler.'

If anyone could rustle up a smuggler, 'O' could. Agar summoned him to a conference. True to form, 'O' assured Agar that he would have no difficulty in finding a smuggler who knew the area better than the Russians themselves. The price of engaging his services would be quite reasonable too—a few bottles of liquor and some tobacco. It seemed that for that fee, the smuggler would be quite prepared to risk his life.

To lessen the possibility of discovery when engaged in his nocturnal trips, Agar aimed to find a base as close as possible to the Russian city. To this end he, 'O' and one of the other agents carried out a reconnaissance, accompanied by an influential Finnish businessman whose sympathies lay with the British. The combined intelligence of his three companions led Agar to choose a quiet little nook, known as Terrioki, which lay barely twelve miles from Kronstadt.

At the head of the small inlet lay a deserted yacht club which had been the haunt of the rich before the war. Now it was infrequently visited by less reputable characters who smuggled loot into Finland from Russia. It was an ideal base for the CMBs with a ready-built harbour and a typically Finnish summer house nearby which could be used as a headquarters. It did however have one disadvantage. Not far from it was a Finnish military outpost and Agar saw clearly that their activities might be observed by the militia manning it. Some 'arrangement' would have to be arrived at with the commandant, Colonel Sarin.

There were two factors in Agar's favour. Sarin was passionately anti-Russian. Furthermore, the wealthy Finnish businessman who accompanied Agar was a man of considerable influence in the upper echelons of the Finnish government. Sarin knew this and when his affluent fellow-countryman approached him on Agar's behalf, he was quite receptive to the idea of Agar's motor boats being kept at the yacht club. But Sarin was nobody's fool and the 'salesman' cover story just did not wash with him. Agar therefore decided to let him into his 'secret'. He told Sarin that he was working for British Intelligence and would be engaged in nothing more serious than observing the movements of the Russian fleet. This satisfied the colonel and he gave his consent but he wanted a piece of the action too and insisted that any information Agar gathered about the Russian fleet should be passed on to him. Agar willingly agreed to this condition and he and his Finnish accomplice left with a promise from Sarin that, when the boats arrived, he would give them a soldier to stand guard over the yacht club and ensure that none of the smugglers whom he knew used the club, would venture near it! Agar was well pleased with the meeting and returned to Helsinki in buoyant mood.

In due course Sindall and the two CMBs arrived at Helsinki but their arrival posed the problem of how to get them to Terrioki without arousing suspicion. Agar realised that if he were to take the boats along the coast they would inevitably be spotted and awkward questions might be asked. But then he discovered that Admiral Cowan had moved his ships to Reval in Estonia and he resolved to ask for his help.

Agar met the British Admiral aboard his flag-ship and the young lieutenant found the Admiral only too willing to be of assistance. He promised to send a destroyer to a point off Helsinki where it would rendezvous with the CMBs. The destroyer would then take them in tow along the coast to a position where an oiler would be waiting to supply them with fuel. When they had taken on as much fuel as they could carry the CMBs would slip into Terrioki under cover of darkness. Agar was delighted with the plan and realised that he had found a very useful ally in Cowan.

The Admiral briefly brought Agar up to date on the political and military situation that existed in the Baltic. These were troubled waters and the atmosphere was tense. There was every likelihood that a spark would ignite the situation and result in a bloody conflict. Cowan's orders were clear; if the Russian fleet left its anchorage at Kronstadt and attempted to interfere with British or friendly shipping in the Baltic then he was to engage it.

As Cowan briefed Agar, the lieutenant sensed that the Admiral's brain was evolving a scheme. In fact the senior officer could see that Agar's boats might well prove valuable in an offensive role if the situation were to take a turn for the worse. After all, they were equipped to take torpedoes—and Cowan had a handsome supply of these. But despite his seniority, Cowan had to be diplomatically cautious. He could see that Agar had no shortage of fighting spirit but, because of the nature of his task, he could not come out directly and ask him to go on the offensive. He decided upon the devious approach . . .

'These little boats of yours *do* carry torpedoes, don't they?' he ventured almost casually.

Agar answered in the affirmative and he was abreast of the Admiral's train of thought. He knew what was coming next. A wry smile came to Cowan's face. The glint in Agar's eyes betrayed his keen interest. Cowan had his man baited. But even so, he dared not press him. Agar was after all working for the Secret Service and the Admiral could be accused of poaching if he were to lure Agar away from his primary task.

'Supposing things were to get really hot here in the Baltic and I did have a crack at the Bolshies. D'you think you might be in a position to lend a hand, without interfering with your other work, of course?'

'We'd be delighted, sir.' Agar said. 'But there is one problem. We haven't any torpedoes.'

'No fish, eh?' the Admiral said thoughtfully. 'You know, Agar, I do believe we have a couple of spares we could *lend* you. We'd want 'em back if you didn't find a use for them, d'you understand?' he said with a grin.

'They certainly would come in handy if we ever got into a tight spot with a Russian warship. You see, we've no means of defence. We don't carry any armament at all but if we had torpedoes at least we'd have a fighting chance.'

'No promises, Agar,' Cowan began, 'but when you meet up with the oiler, you may find that she's got a couple of packages on board for you. Check with her captain when you meet him. Alright?'

That was it. The meeting was over and Agar headed back for Helsinki feeling less 'lonely' than he had done when he first set foot on Finnish soil. Now that he and Cowan had established a rapport, he knew he could count on his help and backing.

Cowan was true to his word. The CMBs made out to sea one evening and met up with the destroyer which took them in tow then headed out to sea in a wide arc before heading inland once more where they found the oiler riding at anchor. When the fuelling-up was completed, two 'special packages' were lowered aboard the CMBs. The packages were wrapped in tarpaulins and such was Cowan's attention to secrecy that none of the sailors who took part in the operation knew what it was all about. The impression in both the oiler and the destroyer was that the civilians who crewed the boats were VIPs and friends of the Admiral. Agar was quite content to leave it like that and under the cloak of darkness, the two boats slipped into the tiny inlet at Terrioki.

Agar's organisation was complete; his boats had arrived, his crews were complete and his contacts were established. Now at last he could carry out the work he had been sent to do.

Two factors, apart from the plight of ST25 in Petrograd, made their mission most urgent. It was already early June and the time was fast approaching when it would be almost continuous daylight, making their nocturnal excursions into Petrograd doubly difficult. But secondly, and tragically, there was a disastrous breakdown in communication between the White Russians who were poised to march on Petrograd and their sympathisers in the fortress of Krasnaya Gorka which stood at the southern entrance to the Gulf of Finland. The Whites in the fortress, thinking that their army had already begun its march, revolted and hoisted their flag—it was the white flag to the red bull. The army had not in fact marched and the fortress stood alone. It was inevitable that the Red Russian fleet would bring its guns to bear on the White outpost. The fleet base at Kronstadt was the scene of chaos and Agar saw his chance of slipping into Petrograd while confusion still reigned. There was no time to be lost.

'O' would be taken across that night and dropped on the coast a little way from the city of Petrograd. Agar concocted a letter to ST25, urging him to return with 'O'. If all went well, 'O' would make contact with ST25 and they would be picked up by Agar on a future trip into Petrograd. The trip would also give Agar the opportunity of observing any movement of the Red fleet.

Agar had to act swiftly in preparation for the night's expedition. 'O' had already recruited a 'navigator' in the unlikely shape of a decidedly dubious-looking character, a creature of the night who had no need of a chart to find his way into Petrograd. He looked every inch the smuggler, unshaven, threadbare and topped by a cap which looked as if it were a permanent fixture and completely immovable. His fee for the night's work was a small sum of money on account, the remainder to be paid upon their return plus two bottles of rum. After some heated bargaining, he agreed to these conditions and seemed well pleased. He assured Agar that there were two safe channels through the breakwaters to Petrograd and pointed out on the chart an ideal landing point for 'O'.

Throughout the day the route was gone over time and time again while 'O' checked his forged identity papers, passes and details of his part in the plan. He was to be dropped at a point off an island which stood at the mouth of the River Neva, then row ashore. Once he had reached the land, he would signal to the CMB by torch indicating that he had landed safely. The whole procedure would be repeated in reverse two nights later and with luck, Cumming's precious agent would be out of danger.

That night, as dusk embraced the tiny inlet, Agar, Beeley, 'O' and the smuggler boarded the CMB. So as not to advertise their departure, they rowed the craft from the harbour and out of the inlet. At a safe distance out into the Gulf, Agar ordered slow ahead and the motor boat crept into the growing darkness. The shore line faded into the gloom behind the CMB and Agar called for more speed, but not enough to cast up a prominent and phosphorescent wake which would betray their presence to any ship in the vicinity. The boat throbbed as it skimmed across the choppy sea. Agar stood at the wheel, his eyes continuously scanning the sea ahead and thrusting forward on a compass course. Meanwhile 'O' and the smuggler sat in the well of the boat while Beeley nursed his engines with loving care, oblivious to the stinging spray that bit his face.

As Agar's boat forged nearer to its goal, the Lieutenant could not help but reflect upon the plight of Cumming's agent in Russia. He knew him only by his code name and Agar pondered upon what kind of man ST25 was and why he risked his life on foreign soil. It was not until much later that he discovered the identity of the man whom he was bent upon rescuing. He was Paul Dukes, a Briton, and perhaps one of the greatest, most daring and resourceful spies ever employed by the Secret Service. Dukes was head of the British Intelligence Service in Russia and set up the organisation shortly after the Revolution. He spoke Russian fluently, having learnt the language while studying music in Moscow before the war. At that time he was already sowing the seeds of his espionage activities by becoming a member of the Communist Party and enlisting in the Red Army. By doing so, he was perfectly placed to collect information which he ferried back to England. Throughout his time in Russia, he escaped death many times, often when engaged upon quixotically chivalrous missions to rescue White Russians from prison. With privileged information he succeeded in penetrating prisons and spiriting away White Russians who were under sentence of death. His fearlessness knew no bounds and his adventures bordered on the reckless. But Dukes had an ace up his sleeve which, fortunately for him, foxed the Reds; he was a master of disguise. His is known to have posed as a proletarian, an epileptic, an ageing intellectual and a card-carrying member of the Communist Party. Had his true identity been revealed to those among whom he circulated, he would have been put to death in a most horrific way. Despite the danger, in which he seemed to revel, he and 'O' stole vast treasures from the Communists, who had helped themselves to the riches of the wealthy. These they smuggled to the Whites who in turn used them in building up their arsenal.

Following the breakdown in the courier service to Finland, Dukes found himself isolated, with a great store of vital information and no way of getting it out. So desperate did the situation become that he was forced to destroy much of it because the chance of discovery was greatly heightened as it accumulated. It was Agar's aim to rectify this dilemma.

Agar jolted himself from his thoughts. The CMB was fast closing the string of forts with their submerged breakwaters. Now was the time for absolute caution. It was here that the smuggler came into play. Agar reduced speed to a crawl as the 'pilot' took the wheel and the CMB nosed between the great black shapes of the forts. The moment was tense and filled with the expectation of a burst of fire. But it did not come and they slid through the gap unmolested. Heaving a deep sigh of relief, they increased speed. Now, with the first barrier behind them, Agar gave his boat more throttle. The boat surged forward, skimming the waves with her bows high in the air and casting out a glowing white wake which streamed out behind her. The CMB fairly trembled as it darted forward with its engines roaring. The wind whipped into the faces of the four men in the cockpit. Soon they would be nearing the gaping mouth of the Neva.

Agar's smuggler seemed to sense by some instinct that they were nearing the point at which 'O' would be dropped and yet there were no points of reference. Their first landmark, the island of Krestovsky, had not yet come into view. How this shabby ruffian knew, Agar did not discover but he was proved correct for, moments later, the dark mass of the island took shape ahead of them.

Agar altered course to take the boat towards the south shore of the Neva. Midnight was only moments away and to Agar it seemed fitting that the climax to their clandestine escapade should be reached at the bewitching hour. He cut speed and nosed in towards the shore line at dead slow until finally he cut engines. The small pram which would take 'O' ashore was lowered over the side. Agar clasped the courier's hand and bade him good luck.

Then, without hesitation, 'O' was on board the pram and rowing off into the darkness. Agar watched him go, marvelling at his courage and wondering if he would ever see him again. The minutes ticked slowly by as they waited for the courier's signal to indicate that he was safely ashore. It seemed like an eternity before finally three distinct flashes could be seen. He'd done it. Now was the time to go.

The CMB made off at thirty knots, retracing its steps until once more, it crept through the gap between the forts without stirring the lookouts. By now the first rays of dawn were lighting the sky and Agar determined to venture a look at the Russian fleet. He rode as near as he dared to Kronstadt and there caught his first sight of the Bolshevik ships. First to come into view were several big warships, then, lying close by, the smaller destroyers. Agar guessed from their position that they could bombard the fortress at Krasnaya Gorka with ease. Indeed it looked as if the ships had moved into position for just that purpose. If that were the case then Agar would have to get that information to London and inform both Cowan and Colonel Sarin as quickly as possible. The Baltic was poised to explode into a bloody holocaust and Agar's actions could well have a profound effect upon how the opening rounds of the impending battle went. He dashed back to Terrioki at top speed.

Agar leapt off the CMB before she was properly berthed and raced to see Sarin. The implications of the Russian fleet movements were not lost upon Sarin who volunteered to pass on the information to Admiral Cowan. The political hot-lines in the Baltic buzzed in a fury of exchanges with frantic pleas from the Whites to the Finns to come to their aid. The Finns were obliged to decline because of domestic problems of their own.

The following day, Agar had a ringside seat atop a church steeple when the bombardment began. It was a trying experience for he felt helpless as Bolshevik shells rained down in a fierce blitz. He remembered the two torpedoes that nestled in their troughs on the CMBs and wished that he could strike a blow at the Red ships but his enthusiasm had to be tempered by the thought of the real purpose of his mission.

That night he was to return to the Neva to pick up 'O' and nothing could be allowed to interfere with that. This however did nothing to lessen the frustration he felt at watching his allies being shelled throughout the morning and the early afternoon until finally the pounding ceased. Sickened by the awful sight he had witnessed, Agar set about the preparations for the night's work.

Just before dusk, Agar's smuggler arrived to earn himself more bounty. But Agar noticed a marked change in the man. He was nervous and perhaps had good reason to be. In the forty-eight hours that had elapsed, the period of night darkness had shortened considerably, making their chances of discovery so much greater. Agar's concern was heightened because there would be no room for manoeuvre if 'O' happened to be late at the rendezvous.

Agar took Hampsheir along with him as an extra hand in case of trouble and when darkness fell they cast off. The CMB traced the same path as it had taken the night before last and to the great relief of all on board they slipped through the forts without trouble. With the aid of the jittery smuggler, Agar brought the CMB to the rendezvous point and cut his engine.

It was a cold night and the wind bit into the four men as they waited expectantly for the flashes of the agent's torch. Their eyes scanned the inky-black shore which was lined by a bank of thick reeds in which 'O' had hidden his pram. The wait seemed interminable as the CMB rocked in the heaving water and the waves lapped against her hull. At last they came, dim but certain, three long flashes.

'O' emerged from the gloom but he was alone in the pram and had to be dragged bodily on board the CMB. He was physically exhausted, wet and bedraggled and he collapsed into the well of the boat. As the boat got under way, a strong tot of brandy revived the courier and he began to relate haltingly the adventure of the past two days.

'O' had succeeded in contacting Paul Dukes but for reasons known only to himself, the spy had declined to come out of Russia. He had however given 'O' some vital documents which were to be passed on to London. Dukes had insisted that no further attempt should be made to get him out until the period of short nights was past. 'O' described how dangerous Dukes' situation really was. At the time of meeting him, Dukes had been hiding out in a spacious tomb where he had a bed and a cache of food. Wandering at large in Russia was a hazardous pursuit. It was common for anyone who appeared in the slightest way suspicious to be shot without trial. In spite of this, Dukes valiantly opted to stay a little longer to complete his work before leaving Russia.

Agar's CMB only just succeeded in squirming through the gap between the forts before dawn finally arrived. As they headed back to Terrioki at speed they could see the ships of the Russian fleet in the distance, clearly standing ready for another bombardment.

When the CMB berthed at Terrioki, Agar was worried. It needed little imagination to appreciate the perilous plight of the White Russians in the fort. The Red Russian fleet could stand and bombard with impunity. It was clear that Admiral Cowan's cruisers would be no match for the Bolsheviks' capital ships. Furthermore, the Reds were screened by minefields and for the British ships these fields were impenetrable. As Agar saw it, there were but two ways of harrying the Bolshevik fleet—either by air attack or by torpedo attack using his own CMBs. He resolved to see Cowan as soon as possible to put a plan of action to him.

Agar knew that Cowan was now operating out of a Finnish port and he approached Colonel Sarin for help with transportation. It was duly provided and Agar sped to Bjorko where Cowan saw him immediately. The Admiral confirmed Agar's fears that there was nothing he could do to attack the Bolshevik ships unless they came out from behind the minefields—and that was unlikely. Agar volunteered to attack the bombarding ships but made it clear that he could not do so without first getting clearance from Mansfield Cumming in London. A secret signal was duly sent and reply came back by return. It was not encouraging. Cumming told him that he was to use his boats for intelligence purposes only unless he was specifically directed to attack by Cowan. Neither of the two men who sat in the cruiser's cabin had expected anything else. For his part, Cowan knew he could not order Agar to carry out the attack but he did assure him that, if he did, he could count on his support.

From Agar's point of view, Cowan's comment was as good as a 'green light' to go ahead and he went back to Terrioki with all speed. He resolved to launch an attack that very night and for what remained of the day the yacht club was a hive of preparatory activity.

Agar judged that the best time to attack would be at 1 a.m. The crews were mustered and briefed and the boats made ready. There was great excitement as they boarded their boats and the two CMBs crept out of the inlet. Once off-shore they donned their uniforms, hoisted White Ensigns and at full throttle charged out to sea.

The boats skimmed at speed towards Kronstadt where the Bolshevik battleships lay. But as they neared the minefields, Sindall's boat suddenly jolted, leapt high in the air then thudded back down onto the waves, casting the crew into the well of the boat. She had hit a floating mine which had broken free of its mooring but miraculously the pronged sphere had not exploded. However, the impact had fractured the propeller shaft and the boat wallowed in the waves with the engine racing and the crew gathering their wits. They were all injured but lucky to be alive. Had the mine exploded there would have been nothing left of the boat or the crew.

Agar swung his boat around and drew alongside Sindall's crippled craft. Piper, Sindall's mechanic, dived overboard and felt his way round to the stern where a blind inspection confirmed the worst—the shaft was broken and he realised that she would need a new one before the CMB could be operational again. It took Agar only a few moments to reach the conclusion that the attack on the Red warships would have to be abandoned. He took Sindall's boat in tow and they made their way back to Terrioki at a crawl, bitterly disappointed at their misfortune. But Agar was not beaten . . .

Back at the yacht club a proper inspection of the damaged boat was carried out. The shaft was beyond repair and they had no spares nor did they have the means of fitting one. This meant that Sindall's boat would have to be towed to Helsinki to have a new one fitted, putting her out of operation for a month at least. Sindall was both disappointed and enraged at his bad luck but Agar determined that he would make up for it . . .

After a brief sleep, Agar rose, revived and rejuvenated with the thought that he would undertake the torpedo attack on the warships using his own boat. The new day had brought fresh enthusiasm despite their reversals of the previous night. Agar summoned his colleagues and told them of his plan. The news had the desired effect and they set about the preparations with a will.

Meanwhile, Agar scrambled to the top of the church tower and raised powerful binoculars to his eyes. Far out to sea he could just make out the Russian ships but they were on the move. The battleships were heading back to Kronstadt. He was joined by Colonel Sarin who made the point that the Russian ships had probably run out of ammunition. Either that or the fortress had surrendered. But his original theory was confirmed when a cruiser, with a destroyer escort, churned through the waves and took up a position where the battleships had been. Although they were not to know it then, she was the Bolshevik cruiser *Oleg*, a ship that was to become inextricably linked with Augustus Agar. From their vantage point, they saw her guns flame into a barrage of fire. It seemed that the gallant defenders in the fortress had not given in and were holding out.

That night Agar's boat (CMB4) nosed out of Terrioki with Agar at the wheel, Hampsheir as his Number One and Beeley keeping a fatherly watch over the engine. Again they used the silent departure technique so as not to arouse the curiosity of the Finns. This was vital because Sarin might well have prevented them from going if he had known what they were about. At last, when they were out of earshot of the coast, Agar asked for slow ahead. Beeley coaxed the engine into life and a low groan signalled its starting.

CMB4 edged forward, hardly disturbing the water until Agar judged it safe to call for more speed. She surged forward like a young colt and ate up the space between them and their first point of reference, the Tolboukin lighthouse. The three men in the boat had already donned their uniforms and the White Ensign flapped in the wind.

As the boat lanced across the sea a wind blew up, making the ride a rough one and giving Agar some cause for concern. If the wind became too violent it might well ruin this mission too. But it remained moderate and posed no problems.

By the time the lighthouse came into view, all three of the crew were soaked from the drenching spray cast up by the boat. But the soaking did nothing to dampen their spirits and as they closed the lighthouse, Agar cut his speed. Already they could just distinguish the dark shapes of the destroyers fussing around the cruiser, screening her from intruders. Agar had to penetrate that screen before he could attack the cruiser. She was a plump target, displacing several thousand tons, but she was heavily armoured and would take some wounding.

CMB4 slipped forward at only a few knots while Hampsheir attended to the torpedo. It was held in the trough by stops which prevented it rolling or sliding out. These stops were removed just before firing but first Hampsheir had to remove the safety pin from the firing cartridge. It was a difficult task in the darkness but he was well experienced in the procedure. Huddled over the slender fish, he began easing out the pin but as he did so, the boat lurched as she hit a wave and Hampsheir accidentally fired the torpedo. Fortunately it was held fast but the sudden lurch shook the ship. Hampsheir, already tensed up, was un-nerved by the shock. Agar could not go to his aid and Beeley could give him only words of encouragement. Inserting another cartridge was a delicate business, especially in a boat pitching and tossing in the sea. Hampsheir's hands shook nervously as he slid in another cartridge and at last he succeeded in doing it but he was badly shaken. All was set for the attack.

Agar's hands gripped the wheel tightly as he drove the CMB towards a gap between two destroyers. All the time he had that awful feeling of impending doom. At any moment they might be seen. Searchlights might blaze and they would become the bulls-eye in an easy target. But the lookouts did not cast their eyes in Agar's direction and the boat slid through without stirring up the hornets' nest.

Now ahead of him, Agar could see the great, dark and splendid shape of the cruiser *Oleg*. Hampsheir cleared the torpedo of the stops as Agar swung the boat stern on to the cruiser. A hiss that seemed to echo across the sea spat out from the fish as it leapt out of the trough and plunged into the water, running true and straight for the cruiser. Agar jammed on full throttle. No need for secrecy now, CMB4 almost pounced as the sudden jolt of energy shot her forward, bows high and stern low in the water. She bolted through the gap between the destroyers, scarring the choppy surface with her foaming wake.

On board the Russian ships, startled sailors gathered their wits as a general alarm was raised. The ear-splitting roar of the engine almost deafened the three men in the CMB but it did not mask the thunder of the violent explosion as the torpedo connected with *Oleg*'s hull. The blast ripped a gash in the hull and tons of water poured through the aperture.

Agar had no time to linger and admire his handiwork or determine the extent of the damage to the *Oleg*. He raced towards the Estonian coast in the hope of fooling the Russians into thinking that he had come from there. By that time, the gunners on the ships had awoken from their confusion and the destroyers opened up at the fleeing boat. Bullets peppered the water while shells sent huge plumes surging skyward. But the gunners' aims were off and soon the CMB was out of range. Only then did Agar venture a glance back to see a gigantic, towering black column of smoke belching from the *Oleg*.

In a remarkably short time, the scene of devastation was far behind Agar and his jubilant crew. They whooped with joy at their success as the boat careered across the sea in a wide, circuitous route back to Terrioki. Dawn was upon the Baltic as CMB4 slipped safely back into the inlet. The expression upon the soaked faces of Agar and his crew foretold the result of the mission. The others who had had to stay behind had seen the flashes from the destroyers' guns and were relieved to find them unscathed.

Hampsheir was in a bad way, suffering from shock which had brought on violent sickness. The other two had suffered nothing more than a good soaking. All three were helped ashore and plied with warming drinks. They were exhausted after their four-hour ordeal and they collapsed into a deep sleep. Agar awoke to a command from Colonel Sarin to report to the Finnish military post. He had expected this and anticipated some awkward questions being asked. When he arrived in the commandant's office, he found Sarin puzzled.

'I have just received a telephone call from the commandant of one of our forts farther down the coast,' he revealed. 'He tells me that there was an explosion in the cruiser *Oleg* last night and she has now sunk.'

Agar's face lit. He realised that he had probably seriously damaged the cruiser. Now he was staggered to learn that she had actually sunk. But his momentary show of delight signalled to Sarin that he knew something more of this.

'My colleague believes that she was sabotaged by her own crew but perhaps you know more about it, my friend.'

Agar hesitated. He recognised that Sarin was probing and was hoping that Agar would come clean. The Finn already suspected that there was more to the Englishman's operation than he cared to admit but he could not pinpoint it.

'I have to tell you, Colonel,' Agar began, 'that I sank the *Oleg*.'

Sarin's mouth fell open. He hardly dared to believe what he had just heard.

'You *what*—?' he stammered.

Agar repeated his revelation a trifle meekly, hoping that his judgement of the colonel had been correct. He had built up a friendship with him and felt that he could trust the Finn. Now this was to be put to the test.

Sarin sat listening in stark disbelief as Agar's story unfolded. However, the young lieutenant took care not to reveal anything about his excursions into Petrograd. Had he done so, Sarin would have had a seizure. As it was he appeared to be in a state of partial shock.

'I just cannot believe it. *You* sank the Oleg with one of these little motor boats? Do you realise what you have done? My country is alive with Bolshevik spies. If they were to discover that your raid was launched from here, the Russians would turn their guns on *us*!'

Sarin's complexion was quite pale. Agar tried to calm him.

'I can assure you, Colonel, that we took every precaution to ensure that the Russians would believe that the raid came from the direction of Estonia. Furthermore, my crew and I were wearing uniform and flying the White Ensign.'

Sarin was puzzled and his furrowed brow showed it.

'What do you mean "uniform and flying the White Ensign"? You are civilians. You are not entitled . . .'

'But we are,' Agar interrupted. 'You see I am Lieutenant in His Majesty's Royal Navy and my companions are likewise officers and men. I am, so to speak, on loan to the Secret Service.'

Sarin's expression changed completely from a look bordering on horror to one of relief. This news greatly lessened the chance of the Russians suspecting the connection between Terrioki and the boats which had launched the attack. But even so, Sarin was still concerned.

'Clearly I cannot reveal any of this to anyone, not even my superiors. It is better that no one else knows of it.'

Agar had been hoping for just such a reaction and knew now that Sarin would keep his word.

'But,' the Finn went on, 'I think it would be best if you left here and moved to Bjorko, for a while at least. If your boats are not here then they are not likely to be discovered by the Bolsheviks. You understand, of course.'

'Naturally,' Agar agreed. 'But before moving house, I must see Admiral Cowan and report to him. I must establish beyond doubt that the *Oleg* was sunk—and that poses something of a problem.'

'Perhaps not,' Sarin said thoughtfully. 'I think I might be able to persuade the commandant of Fort Ino to arrange a flight for you over that area. He has some aircraft and they regularly fly in that direction. Because they bear Finnish markings they are not fired upon by the Bolsheviks. I shall see what I can do. Leave it to me.'

Agar was delighted. He could not have wished for a better ally and before he left, Sarin promised to arrange for transport to take him to Fort Ino.

As he walked back to the yacht club, Agar felt a sense of relief at having shared his secret with the Colonel. Before then he had felt devious because Sarin had proved so helpful. Now a great burden had been lifted from his shoulders. But bad news awaited him back at the yacht club—the fortress at Krasnya Gorka had surrendered. Agar's attack had been in vain. An air of gloom descended upon the assembled Britons. It worsened when they discovered that the defenders in the fortress had been brutally massacred by the Reds after the surrender.

The following day, Agar arrived at the small airfield at Fort Ino and clambered aboard a Junkers aircraft. Soon he was winging his way across the Gulf of Finland. Far off to his left he could see Kronstadt and ahead the fortress he had so desperately tried to save. At the head of its flagstaff the Red flag fluttered and for a moment he pondered upon the horrors that had been enacted there. The small aeroplane swept over the fortifications and Agar could see clearly the victorious Bolsheviks mopping up the devastation caused by their own shells. Agar felt sick.

The Junkers wheeled round over the sea and Agar peered out in a bid to find the *Oleg*. It occurred to him that the reports of her sinking might be untrue. Maybe she had not sunk. There was certainly no sign of her. Then he saw her, lying on her side in shallow water 'like some enormous dead whale', as he later described it. He felt elated at the sight. At least the Reds had lost a major warship and his attack had driven the fleet into the sanctuary of Kronstadt. Perhaps the daring attack had not been in vain after all, for it had achieved some strategic advantage. The Bolsheviks had been given a severe fright.

The short flight had confirmed Agar's success and after he landed, he made for Bjorko to see Cowan. When he arrived there he discovered that the Admiral's fleet was on manoeuvres and would not be back until the following day. This gave him a chance to catch up on some sleep.

Early the next morning the fleet arrived and Agar had a short interview with Cowan who was overwhelmed at the news of the successful attack. He agreed with Sarin's advice that Agar should take the boats to another base and suggested Helsinki, where they could remain until the time was right to return to Terrioki and continue the courier duties.

Back at Terrioki, Agar bade Colonel Sarin farewell. They would meet again in a month's time. Then the two CMBs were towed to Helsinki where Sindall's boat was to undergo repairs.

Agar was in desperate need of a rest. The strain of the operations from Terrioki had taken a severe toll of his mental and physical strength and there were no more operations planned for the next month. Even so, he was to be kept busy. He had several more meetings with Admiral Cowan who had seen the great potential of the CMBs and planned to build up a flotilla of them in the Baltic with the object of carrying out more attacks upon the Russian fleet. This was made easier by a change of mood in the Finnish government. It had given Cowan base and port facilities which would enable him to greatly strengthen his forces.

Cowan evolved a strategy which was many years later to be used very effectively in the Second World War. His intention was set up an air base and have RAF aircraft there to work in consort with the CMBs. Agar was able to put Cowan in the picture as to the types of CMBs available and to add his own touches to the plan by suggesting that the boats could also be used for mine-laying. If a good field could be laid, the Bolshevik fleet would find its exit to the Baltic plugged. This had been the Admiral's aim all along. He wanted the threat of the Russian fleet removed so that he could concentrate upon some trouble that was brewing in the Western Baltic. There some Germans were getting restless and agitating in the Gulf of Riga as well as in Latvia and Lithuania.

While Cowan continued to pore over the troubled waters of the Baltic, Agar had to maintain contact with his agents. During one meeting with his man in Stockholm, he received a personal message of congratulations from Cumming, praising him for his good work and especially for the sinking of the *Oleg*. This news came as a relief to Agar for he had been concerned about Cumming's reactions to his deviation from espionage work. Agar now felt that he had a free hand—and he meant to use it if the opportunity arose.

But not everything was running smoothly. It was clear to him that Hampsheir was far from well. He had not recovered from the shock suffered during the *Oleg* attack; indeed he seemed to be getting progressively worse. He was sent to a sanatorium in Finland for a rest but after a short return to Agar, he had to be sent home. It was a sad parting for Agar.

The first two weeks of July saw the culmination of all the planning. The formation of the new CMB flotilla was taking shape. Boats were on their way to Bjorko from England under tow by RN ships. HMS *Vindictive*, a warship which had been converted into an aircraft carrier with flying-on and flying-off decks, had arrived and was to serve as a depot ship for the sea planes and CMBs when they reached Finland.

Meanwhile Agar's two boats had been completely overhauled and were in fine working shape. He brought them to Bjorko prior to returning to Terrioki. His next trip to Petrograd was due to take place on the night of 18/19 July but before he left he had a last meeting with Cowan and got some stirring news . . .

The Admiral was a man of action and already he had devised a plan for attacking the warships at their anchorage at Kronstadt. He aimed to use both the CMBs and a squadron of aircraft. The CMBs under their leader, Commander C. C. Dobson, were due at Bjorko soon, along with the aircraft. When they arrived the plan would be finalised. Cowan asked if Agar would be willing to take on the task of pilot for the attacking force. He willingly agreed and offered to recruit some of his smuggler friends to help. With the brief outline of the plan complete, Agar made to take his leave of the Admiral, but Cowan had not finished . . .

'One last thing, Agar. I ought to tell you that I have recommended you for the award of the Victoria Cross. I think you deserve it. You may not get it, of course, but I wanted you to know I thought you worthy of the recommendation.'

Agar was staggered. The thought of any award for his work in the Baltic had never occurred to him. But he left the Admiral's cabin a very proud man.

Agar duly arrived back at Terrioki with a difficult task ahead of him. So far he had told Sarin only of his Intelligence work and the attack on the *Oleg*. But now he was faced with a problem. More couriers had been recruited and their presence at Terrioki heightened the chances of Sarin discovering the most secret part of Agar's activities. The Englishman realised that if this were to happen by chance then it might throw Sarin into a fury and ruin the operation. After considerable thought and bearing in mind the new and more friendly attitude of the Finnish government, Agar decided to tell Sarin the whole truth. A meeting was arranged.

When Agar told Sarin that he had been running a ferry service for spies between Finland and Petrograd, Sarin's expression was one of anger and for a moment Agar thought that he had made a wrong move. But after due thought, Sarin realised that he was in the presence of a very courageous man and wished him good fortune with his missions. Now Sarin knew everything and Agar promised to keep him informed of his activities.

Over the next few days, both CMBs made trips into Petrograd to ferry in couriers who were to help Paul Dukes with the mountain of stolen documents he was to smuggle out. But although the trips were made without discovery, the couriers did not fare so well and there were some hair-raising incidents. One of them was discovered shortly after being put ashore and only just managed to escape. He succeeded in avoiding capture and for five days trekked to the border of Estonia from where he was brought to Terrioki just in time to warn Agar of what had happened. There was no doubt that the landing area would now be patrolled, so another suitable place had to be found.

This agent was also able to tell Agar that Dukes now proposed leaving Russia on one of two dates, the 4th or 8th of August. He had spent the last few weeks in Moscow which was less of a hot-bed than Petrograd where the Bolsheviks were carrying out a systematic massacre of those suspected of White sympathies.

Sindall had made his first attempt at reaching Petrograd but the forts were on the alert and he only just succeeded in escaping destruction when the guns opened up on him. But his second attempt was successful and he landed his agent.

Amid all this activity Agar learned that the Russian fleet had been active. Cowan had lost a destroyer to a Red submarine and in retaliation he launched an air attack upon the Russian's submarine depot ship. Angered by the loss of one of his ships, he summoned Agar to the flag ship.

When Agar arrived at Bjorko he saw to his delight that the CMB flotilla had arrived and the 55-foot-long boats were moored neatly alongside *Vindictive*. To Agar it was an impressive sight and one that filled him with particular pride because he had helped to build up the base at Osea from where they had come.

In Cowan's cabin, he met Commander Dobson and his second-in-command, Lieutenant Bremmer. They immediately got down to finalising the plan of attack with Squadron Leader Donald, who was in command of the aircraft that were to take part. Agar again volunteered to bring a boat and a smuggler to act as pilots for the raid. This was eagerly accepted by the newcomers who pointed out that there would be a short delay while they carried out a dummy run. Cowan, eager to strike at the Bolsheviks, found the necessity for delay very tiresome and said so but soon realised that the success of the whole operation might be forfeited if a practice were not carried out.

Excited at the prospect of another crack at the Reds, Agar returned to Terrioki to prepare for the evacuation of Paul Dukes from Russia. The preparations were momentarily interrupted by the arrival of a General Signal which read:

'For sinking the Bolshevik cruiser *Oleg* H.M. the King has been pleased to make the following awards. To Lieutenant Agar RN the Victoria Cross. To Acting Sub-Lieutenant Hampsheir RNR the Distinguished Service Cross. To Chief M M Beeley RNVR the Conspicuous Gallantry Medal.'

Confirmation of the award of Britain's highest medal for valour had arrived but when the announcement was made in the newspapers at home, no mention was made of how it had been won. The veil of secrecy which screened the activities in the Baltic was drawn tight and it was to be much later before these events were told to the public.

Agar's natural delight at the award could not be allowed to interrupt the job in hand and as arranged two more visits were made to Petrograd to pick up Dukes but there was no sign of him on either trip. Agar put 'O' ashore with instructions to Dukes to try again on the 23rd or 25th of August. But before these dates, the CMBs were to take part in an action which is even today hailed as an epic in small boat operations.

Cowan's plan was for a concerted night attack upon the Red warships *inside* the Kronstadt dockyard basin by both CMBs and aircraft. The CMBs were to be split into two groups; one piloted to the target by Agar and the other brought in by Dobson, with the aid of a smuggler. Shortly before the CMB attack, Donald's aircraft would bomb the basin in the hope that the Russian gunner attention would be diverted toward the air, giving the CMBs a better chance of a surprise attack from the sea. To add further weight, a support group of large warships would give all the help they could from outside the minefields. That was the plan in a nutshell and the finer points of detail were left to Dobson and Donald.

Dobson divided the attacking force into two groups of three for the actual attack inside the basin with a seventh boat designated the task of sinking a destroyer guardship at the mouth of the basin. Agar's small CMB, although armed with a torpedo, was primarily there for navigational purposes and was to attack targets other than those already allotted to the others.

During the days preceding the attack, regular reconnaissance flights over Kronstadt kept a weather eye open for any movements of the Bolshevik fleet. On the 17th, Dobson, Donald and Bremmer made a final flight to see for themselves. There were some rich pickings to be had in the basin. Two battleships, the *Andrei Perosvanna* and the *Petropavlosk*, together with the submarine depot ship *Pamiat Azova*, were to be the prime targets with the cruiser *Ruvik* as an alternative.

Bremmer would go in first, followed by Dobson then a third boat under the command of Lieutenant Dayrell-Reed. Bremmer's target would be the submarine depot ship, Dobson would go for the *Petropavlosk* and Dayrell-Reed the *Andrei Perosvanna*. While these attacks were underway, Lieutenant Napier would attack the destroyer guardship. The three other boats would then charge in to cause further havoc. There was little doubt in any of their minds that the dockyard basin would be chaotic, with CMBs trying to manoeuvre at speed in the confined space, and the danger of collision would be great. The commanders of the boats would require all the skill they could muster.

The success of the mission hinged to a very large extent upon the element of surprise and it was Agar's job to ensure that the boats got to Kronstadt undetected. On the evening of the 17th, Lieutenant Sindall, Marshall, Beeeley and a smuggler set off ahead of the others in their CMB. They were to rendezvous with the flotilla at midnight off Inoneni Point and Agar's boat arrived there with time to spare.

A little before midnight the men on board detected a low drone of approaching engines. It was the flotilla. Agar's boat shook as the engine burst into life and he swept into the lead to take his section on its way. In the darkness the two sections lost sight of each other and Dobson's smuggler took the boats through a gap in the forts which had not previously been used by the CMBs. Agar however used a tried and tested route but as they nosed past a fort they were spotted and fired on by machineguns. But they squirmed through and the firing died. It had not occurred to the Bolsheviks that a raid on their anchorage was imminent so the element of surprise was preserved when the boats finally approached Kronstadt.

The sky was dark and cloudy, which helped to prevent the oncoming boats being seen from the shore. As they neared the yawning entrance RAF aircraft began their blitz. The small bombs plummeted down on Kronstadt and with screaming whistles they erupted in violent explosions throwing the scene into stark relief. The Russians strained their eyes skywards to find their attackers, little suspecting the approaching attack from the sea.

Apart from Agar's boat, all the others carried two torpedoes apiece and they were about to subtract a sizeable piece from the Bolshevik fleet. As searchlights swept the sky, Bremmer's CMB shot through the fifty-yard wide gap and into the basin. From the glare of the searchlights and small fires he saw his target, the submarine depot ship. By the time he was seen, his two torpedoes were already lancing through the water. He brought his boat around and hid in the shadows to allow Dobson into the basin. Moments later the *Pamiat Azova* lurched as both torpedoes struck and exploded, ripping her apart. She sank immediately.

Dobson bolted into the basin and loosed two torpedoes at the battleship *Petropavlosk*. They too found their mark and Dobson slid into the shadows making way for Dayrell-Reed who had to face a fierce barrage of fire from assorted guns on ships and shore. He raced in, made a hairpin turn to shape up for firing at the *Andrei Perosvanna*, but became the focus of a hail of fire. A bullet hit Dayrell-Reed who dropped over the wheel, throwing the boat wildly off course. Lieutenant Gordon Steele who was poised to fire the boat's torpedoes, leapt up from his position and took the wheel. He brought her round despite the fusillade of bullets thrashing his boat and fired two torpedoes. Two great explosions told him that they had hit the battleship.

By now Dobson was heading out of the basin with Steele on his tail, both boats raking the guardship destroyer with machinegun fire. Napier had already made his attack on the destroyer but his torpedoes went wild and as he bolted away, Napier's boat was hit by a shell and ripped in half. Both halves of the CMB sank immediately.

Lieutenant Brade's boat hurtled through the gap but as luck would have it, Bremmer's boat was in the process of clearing the basin at that moment. Collision was inevitable and Brade's boat rammed the other, locking the two together. With great presence of mind, Brade put on speed, keeping the boats in a clinch, and forced the tangle out of the entrance. Once free of it, Brade took Bremmer and his crew on to his boat and wriggled free before the damaged boat was destroyed by a scuttling charge.

Brade still had his two torpedoes and he was determined to use them. He aimed them at the guardship destroyer but they both missed. Guns on the destroyer pumped shells at its attacker and the boat was hit and sunk, killing the gallant Brade and wounding Bremmer.

One boat had failed to reach Kronstadt while another commander had had to abandon his attack when his torpedo firing mechanism jammed. Agar finding the basin impenetrable fired his torpedo into a group of auxiliary vessels moored in a secondary dockyard. With that he joined the remaining boat to struggle back to the forts.

Of the eight boats which took part in the raid, only four returned, having survived the hell of that attack. Both Steele and Dobson were awarded the Victoria Cross. Agar was admitted to the Distinguished Service Order. The raid had been an unqualified success. Both the battleships had sunk, as had the submarine depot ship. In his account of these events, Agar played down the part he played in it. There can be absolutely no doubt that without his inspiration that raid would never have taken place. Cowan owed him a great debt—and he told him so—but, although he was no longer required with the flotilla, Agar had still to get Dukes out of Russia.

He returned to Terrioki where some disturbing news awaited him. It appeared, according to information brought out of Russia that when Agar last went to the rendezvous point off the coast, Paul Dukes had been there! Dukes had rowed out with another courier and could actually see the CMB but his boat had developed a leak and sank. Dukes and his companion had almost drowned before scrambling ashore.

Such misfortune reinforced Agar's determination to make one last effort to get Dukes out. It appeared that for political reasons, it was crucial that he reached London. But Agar's previous route through the forts was no longer as easy as it had been. The Bolsheviks were on the alert, sweeping the sea with searchlights throughout the hours of darkness. Now the chances of being spotted were very much greater than they had been before. But London had been quite explicit—the trip was to be made, whatever the risk.

The night of the last trip was the 23rd/24th of August. If this were not successful then Dukes would have to make his way out of Russia via the long and dangerous route across the Estonian border. Agar was prepared to risk everything to ensure that he got the most important spy in Asia home.

The difficulty that was to face them was highlighted in a dramatic way when two Bolshevik aircraft dropped several bombs in the area around Terrioki. The only casualties were trees but the incidents served to alienate some of the local Finns. So much so that two hand grenades were thrown into the garden of Agar's headquarters. They did little damage but the meaning was clear enough.

Agar set off with Beeley, Marshall, an agent and a smuggler in the CMB to run the gauntlet of the Russian forts. To do so, they would have to dodge at least two searchlight beams. This last voyage was to be the very worst of all—and the most hopeless. No sooner had the boat reached the forts than it was caught in the beams of light. The effect was immediate; guns opened up on them, lashing the sea around the boat. Agar wheeled the CMB around in a crazy gyration of movements to squirm clear of the light and the guns but he was held fast. He swung her round towards Terrioki, hoping to wrest her free for another attempt but in doing so, he got hopelessly lost. He dared not slow down or the shells from the Russian guns would certainly find the boat. The CMB rocketed around in a wide arc but when Agar spun the wheel to change direction the boat simply continued on its course oblivious to his command. One of the rudder ropes had snapped and now the boat was careering around in increasingly large circles. It seemed only a matter of time now before a shell would catch and blast the little boat out of the water. The sea, lit by searchlights, was a boiling cauldron, stirred by exploding shells.

In the near distance, Agar could just make out the island of Kronstadt looming up ahead. He was powerless to alter the boat's course and she bolted towards the growing black mound of land. As she did so, she was quite suddenly engulfed in darkness. The CMB was so close to the island that the searchlights could not depress low enough to find her. The sudden change from light to dark 'blinded' Agar but the boat continued to roar forward at forty knots. A moment later, it hit a rock and stopped dead. Agar hit the wheel and controls in front of him while the others were cast into the well of the cockpit.

Stunned and dazed by the impact, the crew struggled drunkenly to their feet. Marshall was the first to regain complete control of his faculties. He tended to his comrades, finding that none was seriously injured, then he revived them with a tot of rum.

The strong spirit brought the life back to Agar and he examined the boat. She had stuck fast on a rocky breakwater and the sea was pouring into her through a ragged gash in her hull. Each of the men on board took off his leather jacket and plugged up the tear in the wooden hull. Luckily this stemmed the inflow of water which was now reduced to a trickle. But although they had almost stopped the water coming in there seemed little point in carrying on. The boat was stuck on the underwater rock and they were at least fifteen miles from Terrioki. Between them and their base lay the Russian forts—and dawn was only three hours away. Their situation was desperate but Agar was determined not to give in.

By rocking the CMB and pushing with poles, they managed to free the crippled boat from the rock but the engine refused to start and nothing Beeley did could coax it into life. It was then that, by some miracle, the searchlights went out. The Russians clearly thought that the CMB had escaped. Now Agar could concentrate upon getting them out of the mess they were in.

He set about collecting as much canvas as he could find and fashioning it into an improvised sail. Meanwhile Beeley and Marshall baled for their lives with empty petrol cans. Some more cans lashed together at the end of a rope provided a sea anchor. Agar hoisted the sail and a heavy swell and a generous wind caught it and slowly took the boat along. They were under way but there was a long way to go.

Helped along by the swell, the CMB drifted away to the north east. For the next three hours, they baled furiously as the boat made a mere two knots. When dawn finally came, they had sailed only six miles but at least by then they were out of the range of the Russian guns.

It was while they were watching the forts slowly receding into the distance that they saw the two boats closing in on them. They were sail-driven fishing boats and they ploughed through the waves towards the CMB. But when they got within hailing distance, their crews found themselves gaping down the business end of a rapid-fire machinegun on the CMB. Agar's agent passed on his message—'Hand over your sails or we fire!' There was no hesitation on the part of the Russians and soon the sails were taking the CMB swiftly across the Gulf towards Terrioki.

The CMB arrived at Terrioki shortly before mid-day. Their flight across the Gulf had taken twelve hours.

After the trial and tension of that night Agar learned that the whole venture had been in vain—Paul Dukes was already on his way to the border of Estonia with 'O'.

Agar's work at Terrioki was finished and he received orders from London to come home. But before doing so, he could not resist the temptation to carry out just one last mission. He took a CMB to Kronstadt and laid mines, sealing the Russian fleet in. The destroyer guardship which had survived the Kronstadt raid subsequently came to grief on one of Agar's mines. It was a fitting end to a remarkable episode in the Baltic.

Master-spy Paul Dukes, whom Agar had tried so bravely to rescue, arrived in London with his precious documents and was later knighted for his services.

As for Agar, he reached London and once more negotiated the

corridors of the building where Mansfield Cumming waited for him. Nothing had changed, he realised, when he opened the door to the suite of offices—not even the reluctant half-smile on the secretary's face. After all, to her, one spy was much the same as another.

Bibliography

The Longest Day, Cornelius Ryan (Victor Gollancz, 1971)
Great War Adventures, Ed. Leonard Gribble (Arthur Barker, 1966)
Fighting Men, Ed. Patrick Pringle (Evans Bros., 1964)
The Watery Maze, Bernard Fergusson (Collins, 1961)
Wings of Neptune, Donald Macintyre (Peter Davis, 1963)
Duel of Eagles, Peter Townsend (Weidenfeld & Nicolson, 1969)
The Catafighters, Kenneth Poolman (William Kimber, 1970)
The Secret Invaders, Bill Strutton & Michael Pearson (Hodder & Stoughton, 1959)
A History of the British Secret Service, Richard Deacon (Frederick Muller, 1969)
Footprints in the Sea, Augustus Agar (Evans Bros., 1961)
Commando, Peter Young (Macdonald)
The Phantom Major, Virginia Cowles (Collins)
The Raiders; Desert Strike Force, Arthur Swinson (Macdonald)
Evidence in Camera, Constant Babington-Smith (David & Charles, 1974)
Poland, SOE and the Allies, Josef Garlinski (Allen & Unwin, 1969)
The Special Air Service, Philip Warner (William Kimber, 1971)
Secrets and Stories of the War (The Readers Digest, 1963)
German Secret Weapons—Blueprint for Mars, Brian Ford (Macdonald, 1970)
Q Boat Adventures, Harold Auten (Herbert Jenkins)
My Mystery Ships, Gordon Campbell (Hodder & Stoughton, 1928)
The World's Greatest Spies, Charles Wighton (Odhams, 1962)
The Battle for Twelveland, Charles Whiting (Leo Cooper, 1975)
The World of Espionage, Bernard Newman (Souvenir Press, 1962)